"Anyone who wishes to come to a fuller understanding of Jesus and of the Good News he came to proclaim will profit from these meditations. They will be especially useful for the homilist who has the privilege of preaching the gospel every Sunday."

FR. WILLIAM BERGEN, SJ, SENIOR PRIEST, CHURCH OF ST. IGNATIUS LOYOLA, NEW YORK CITY

"Leo Gafney gives us hope that the cultural milieu of division and conflict can be overcome with the love and grace preached in the Christian gospels. This book is a gift to a hurting world. Read it and allow yourself to be transformed!"

REV. DR. DIANE MONTI-CATANIA, UNITED CHURCH OF CHRIST MINISTER

"A fresh look at the gospels! Leo Gafney has done a marvelous job of weaving together Scripture and examples from the saints. The end result is a volume of inspiration and wisdom that makes the gospels pertinent for our present times."

MARGE STEINHAGE FENELON, AUTHOR OF *10 PROMISES OF JESUS: STORIES AND SCRIPTURE REFLECTIONS ABOUT SUFFERING AND JOY*

"In this book Jesus becomes more human in his words and more divine in his actions. It is an excellent text for study groups or even individuals who wish to deepen their appreciation of Scripture while enriching their own spiritual lives. This book helps us to understand who Jesus is and who we are in responding to his message of love."

RICHARD CROGHAN, THOMAS MERTON SCHOLAR AND RETIRED EDUCATOR FROM THE UNIVERSITY OF NEW MEXICO

D0840849

"How beautifully Leo Gafney leads us to cultivate a deeper relationship with God. By provoking reflections and suggested practices, Leo encounters God imaginatively and leads us to contemplate what it would it take of me to become closer to God."

JEANNE WARDELL, CATHOLIC YOUTH INSTRUCTOR,
ST. MARTIN OF TOURS PARISH, LAKEVILLE, CT

"With this book, Leo Gafney clears the way for the person of faith to come face to face in prayer with Jesus Christ. No small gift! By adopting the pace and tone presented in these pages, the willing reader can experience the presence of God in prayer."

WILLIAM J. BYRON, SJ, AUTHOR OF A BOOK OF QUIET PRAYER

"One of the more exciting elements of this work is Leo Gafney's attention to the week rather than the day. His shift to the weekly rhythms provides a more realistic framework for students, making spiritual life feel a whole lot more accessible."

LYNN A. COOPER, CATHOLIC CHAPLAIN, TUFTS UNIVERSITY,
THE INTERFAITH CENTER

"Those who wish to consider in prayer the words spoken by Jesus in the New Testament will find fresh insights and challenges in this accessible book. It is designed not for a quick read but as a source for prayer over twenty-five weeks. Both quiet persons in the pew and those whose duties involve preaching in word as well as work will find guidance for prayer here."

GEORGE BUR, SJ, SUPERIOR OF THE JESUIT COMMUNITY OF
ST. ISAAC JOGUES, WERNERSVILLE, PA

WHO DO YOU SAY THAT I AM?

Conversations with Jesus in the Gospels

LEO GAFNEY

TWENTY-THIRD
PUBLICATIONS
twentythirdpublications.com

Twenty-Third Publications
One Montauk Avenue, Suite 200
New London, CT 06320
(860) 437-3012 or (800) 321-0411
www.twentythirdpublications.com

The Scripture passages contained herein are from the *New Revised Standard
Version Bible*, Catholic edition. Copyright ©1989, by the Division of
Christian Education of the National Council of the Churches of Christ in
the U.S.A. All rights reserved.

Cover image: © iStockphoto.com / aytacbicer

ISBN: 978-1-62785-487-0
Printed in the U.S.A.

 A division of Bayard, Inc.

Contents

Part II

Jesus Responds

Part III

Jesus Is in Charge

INTRODUCTION

The gospels are so rich in meaning that we must meditate and pray over them phrase by phrase. This book focuses on brief encounters between Jesus and another person or small group. Someone asks a question and Jesus responds, or the reverse. Jesus considers the person with whom he speaks, the circumstances, his own views, and his mission. One person asks to be cured; John the Baptist asks if Jesus is the one who is to come; Jesus asks Peter what people are saying about him. In these and many other encounters, Jesus' replies, his questions, and his comments will engage and perhaps surprise us.

We should place ourselves in the story. In one curious incident, Jesus calls to his disciples from the shore, telling them to fish from the other side of the boat. Did he have some special knowledge? Or perhaps he saw a school of fish. What might this mean to us? Perhaps there are times when we should try something different.

We should also be alert to the presence of God in these encounters. Jesus' thoughts, captured in his words and exchanges, bring new perspectives. Like his parables and like the Beatitudes, his exchanges with people give us glimpses into that mysterious world that he inhabits with the Father.

In this book, I have offered examples from Scripture and from the lives of Christians to suggest different ways in which we might respond to the gospels. Jesus continues speaking to us. He is fully divine but also human beyond our expectations.

And how are we to respond to Jesus when we encounter him? We must realize that each encounter is personal and also communal. God reaches out to us every day, in every part of our lives. Jesus is our guide and our connection to God— that mystery deep within and also far beyond us. Prayer and meditation help because they open the door to the Spirit who gives the light and the warmth we need in our encounters with God.

This book is arranged for use on a weekly basis. The Scripture verses that start each chapter can help focus the mind, and a weekly practice is suggested at the conclusion of each chapter.

PART I

JESUS ASKS A QUESTION

Jesus asked questions not to gain information or guidance. He asked questions so that people would stop and think. As Christians, we attach ourselves to Christ. And as we read and pray over the gospel passages, he asks you and me the same questions. "Who do you say that I am?" "What do you want me to do for you?" "Where is your faith?" So it is that Jesus speaks to us, across the centuries and languages and circumstances. And he waits for us to respond.

In these gospel situations we consider how Jesus immerses himself in the lives of those around him and at the same time lifts them with him to the life he shares with the Father. We also consider how some exemplary Christians responded, how Jesus changed them, and how they can help us answer Jesus' questions.

Coming of Age

*"Child, why have you treated us like this? Look, your
father and I have been searching for you in great
anxiety."..."Why were you searching for me? Did you
not know that I must be in my Father's house?"*

[LUKE 2:48-49]

J ust before this exchange we read that the family had
traveled to Jerusalem for the Passover feast, as they did
every year, and that Jesus at this time was twelve. Those
who are parents or have had charge of children know what
it is like to lose a child, even for a short time. We feel "great
anxiety," just as Jesus' mother says. We panic and our imagi-
nations run wild, considering what might have happened. For
most of us the loss is brief; we are united again, and we are
happy together.

And so it is easy to transfer Jesus' situation to today's
world and consider what happened. Imagine an outing with
families traveling in three or four buses. The group gets
together for the trip home. There are extended families and
parents talking with friends. Parents of a child board different buses; each assumes that the child is with the other; he
has been with them for the whole trip. After several hours the

buses come to a rest stop and the discovery is made. "Where is he?" the parents ask one another, and their concerns grow. Of course, they must go back.

But in the story, as Luke describes it, it was only "after three days," that they found Jesus in the temple. Imagine the first nightfall not finding him. What do they think and fear? We know from Jesus' own stories that there were robbers in and around Jerusalem—although he would not have had much to be stolen. There was also the Roman army, which like any army had the good and the bad. We know this from the way they are portrayed in the gospels and the way they treated Jesus in his final hours. Where did Jesus stay; what did he eat? It does seem that the culture of Israel at that time was welcoming and caring, and people often slept outdoors. And at Passover time the population of Jerusalem swelled to four or five times its normal size. Jesus undoubtedly found friendly people. And although only twelve, he would have been nearing adult status.

In any case, Jesus did survive the three days. He did much more than survive. Perhaps it was a "coming of age" experience—in part to find his independence and freedom, but, more important, to encounter God.

We read that they found Jesus in the temple among the elders, asking them questions. Jesus wanted to understand how God works among his people. Perhaps he asked about the words of Isaiah, "he was despised and rejected by others; a man of suffering and acquainted with infirmity." We know from Jesus' life and teaching that he had compassion for those in need and expected his own life to end early with suffering and death.

Perhaps he asked the elders about the Passover prayers and observance of the Shabbat.

Blessed are You, God our God, King of the universe, who makes a distinction between sacred and profane, between light and darkness, between Israel and the nations, between the seventh day and the six workdays. [SHABBAT BLESSING PRAYER]

We know that Jesus observed the prayers and customs of his people, but he also created controversy when he healed on the Sabbath. The story also says that those around him in the temple were amazed at his answers. Perhaps Mary and Joseph were also amazed; but they were anxious. The gospel tells us that he went back to Nazareth and was obedient to them.

THE CHRISTIAN EXPERIENCE

St. Francis of Assisi recognized God's call while coming of age. Francis celebrated life with his friends, as young people often do—having fun, drinking, and partying. Then he wanted to be a knight and spent a great deal of his father's money on a suit of armor. Finally, he had several dreams and visions:

"Where are you going?"
"To Apulia, to become a knight."
"Now tell me, Francis, which of the two would be of greater advantage to you, the master or the servant?"
"The master!"
"Why then do you leave the master for the sake of the servant, the prince for the vassal?"

While at prayer, Francis also heard a voice saying, "Francis, repair my church." He thought the instruction was to rebuild a nearby abandoned church building. But gradually he came to understand that repair was needed for the whole church, the people more than the buildings. The institutional church in many ways did not reflect what Christ had taught and lived.

Francis chose poverty as the center of his life and worship. He and his followers were to own nothing—no extra clothes, no money, not even books. He, like many before and since, found that "things" did not provide freedom and security. Rather, the desire and need for things enslaves us. It is because, once we begin wanting and needing, we always want more. Francis's independence and freedom took root in his soul because he did not want things or need money.

Jesus, staying behind in Jerusalem, was exercising a degree of independence from his parents. How many "coming of age" stories have we read? There may be some special event—war, work, love, and even family disruption—that precipitates the initial separation from family. That separation may be one of real distance; or it may be psychological. Young people must begin to find their own way. Each of us has at some time, or through a number of experiences, separated ourselves from our parents. It is part of life.

When we leave home, the culture and safety of our early life produces both anxiety and exhilaration. We may come closer to God, or we may wander. Like Jesus, we are likely to come home—perhaps many times—to those we love. Like Jesus, we will also go out on our own, taking with us the love of our home life.

REFLECTION

In our personal growth and as Christians, we might "come of age" more than once during our lives. At the end of the story we have been considering—of Jesus when he was twelve—the gospel says that he "increased in wisdom and in years." This is not just pious talk. Jesus did grow in his understanding of God's work in his life—and so should we. Consider as you read this, your age, your commitments, your work or studies. In what ways is God calling on you to come of age, to grow, once more? Only you know the answer. God is not asking the impossible. But God wants you to let the knowledge and example of his image, Christ our Lord, live more fully in your mind and heart. He left home; he questioned the teachers in the temple. What questions are you asking about the next steps in your life?

WEEKLY PRACTICE

Picture Jesus talking with his mother. Consider how Jesus learned and came of age by taking on new responsibilities and meeting new people. Each day, write down what God might be calling you to do next. You don't have to do everything on the list, but pray and listen to the Holy Spirit who may be calling you to come of age one more time.

Good reflection. Nothing that diminishes the authority or integrity of Scripture. Offers a meditation through the perspective of Jesus rather in addition to the more typical view of Mary & Joseph.

≈ 2 ≈

To Touch
the Lord

*She had heard about Jesus, and came up behind him
in the crowd and touched his cloak, for she said, "If I
but touch his clothes, I will be made well." Immediately
her hemorrhage stopped; and she felt in her body that
she was healed of her disease. Immediately aware that
power had gone forth from him, Jesus turned about in
the crowd and said, "Who touched my clothes?" And his
disciples said to him, "You see the crowd pressing in on
you, how can you say, 'Who touched me?'"*

[MARK 5:27–31]

As the Gospel of Mark moves forward, we get the
sense that Jesus is propelled by events but also in
control of each situation. The healing described
above is folded within a larger story of Jesus raising a girl
from death.

But let us reflect on the narrative. When political leaders travel, they surround themselves with security person-
nel. Even in ancient times access to those in authority was
restricted. Depictions of Jesus often show him at some dis-

tance from the others, dressed in white, tall and handsome, with a well-trimmed beard. Is that what it was like?

Michael Casey suggests a rather different portrait. He surmises that Jesus, as a first-century, Middle-Eastern man approaching middle age, may have been—by our standards—on the short side, balding, perhaps putting on some weight.

As noted above, Jesus did not stand out from the crowd. This is reinforced by the comment and question from his disciples pointing out that Jesus is surrounded by people, and they are constantly touching him. He didn't mind; that was the way life was. People were familiar and comfortable enough with Jesus to point this out: How can you ask who touched you? We are always touching one another.

I recall reading about a sociological study comparing different cultural habits regarding touching. They looked at families picnicking and the number of times they touched one another in an hour. The results were something like: English, ten times; American, twenty-five times; Hispanic, two hundred times. Touching is important to all of us, but more common in some cultures than others.

Anyway, this touch that Jesus noted was more than the common touch of communication or friendship. In Luke's account, Jesus says, "I felt power go out from me."

We are also told that the woman had been afflicted for twelve years and had spent all her money seeking cures, but her condition grew worse. Did she turn to Jesus out of desperation? Perhaps that was part of it, but Jesus told her, as he often did, that her faith had made her well.

The incident and the woman's simplicity remind us of another gospel verse: "Amen, I say to you, unless you be converted and become as little children, you shall not enter into the kingdom of heaven" (Matthew 18:3). The woman was perhaps desperate, but something in her had changed; she turned in simplicity to the one in whom she saw goodness and compassion.

THE CHRISTIAN EXPERIENCE

This then reminds us of St. Thérèse of Lisieux, who has become a shining example of the value in doing little things with love, bringing ourselves close to Jesus, touching him in spirit. She also wondered why it was that some were favored or called or cured and why some people went through their whole lives without having heard the name of Jesus. She answered the question herself.

> Jesus deigned to teach me this mystery. He set before me the book of nature; I understood how all the flowers He has created are beautiful, how the splendor of the rose and the whiteness of the lily do not take away the perfume of the little violet or the delightful simplicity of the daisy. I understood that if all the flowers wanted to be roses, nature would lose her springtime beauty, and the fields would no longer be decked out with little wild flowers.

St. Thérèse became known as the Little Flower, symbol of simplicity. She learned and taught the value of turning our lives over to God in small ways, one step at a time. She is also well known for her belief that her real mission was to begin with her death. We all believe that this is true for Jesus Christ. His redemptive death brought God's love in a special way. But even with our best efforts to believe, most of us believe that our one chance is here and now, not after death.

But St. Thérèse wrote about herself.

> I feel that I am going to my rest...but above all, I feel that my mission is about to begin, my mission of making God loved as I love him, of giving my little way to other souls. If God grants my request, my Heaven will be spent on earth, until the end of the world. Yes, I wish to spend my Heaven in doing good on earth.

We should pray often to have such simple faith and hope in our life, continuing after death. The woman who was cured in the narrative we are considering has only that brief moment in the gospels, but she remains strong in the memory of Christians. With millions who have come before us we believe that we can come close to Jesus, and we will feel his healing power, based in part on that woman's faith.

As Christians we should be willing and able to believe that we will continue to do good even after we die. How does that happen? It happens in many ways. As a parent or teacher or coworker or friend the positive things we do will continue after our lives end. But St. Thérèse meant something more than this. She meant that as part of the body of Christ she would continue to be involved and engaged with the people of this world—through the words she left behind and through her real interventions from beyond. The same will be true of us.

We are connected to one another in Christ; and we will remain connected. Jesus has touched each of us and we can touch others with his love and healing power. We should let others come into our lives and touch us. Healing power may even go out from us without our knowing it.

REFLECTION

The modern world tells us in many ways that we should strive to be noticed, to be different, to stand out. Jesus tells us something else. He blended in with the crowed. He accepted the pushing and shoving of everyday life. Yes, his teaching lifts us close to God. But in living that teaching we are to be in the crowd. In how many ways do you try to stand out, to be special? You are indeed special in God's plan. And we as a people have a special mission; that mission will take us, seamlessly, from this world to the next.

WEEKLY PRACTICE

Try to accept and appreciate the needs of those around you as Christ accepted and was attentive to the woman following him. We often miss those who would like a word of encouragement, a phone call, or a visit. We, through Christ, have more love and energy to share than we know.

+ Good reflection again. Ties in with St. Thérèse.

− Little concern with the possible description of Jesus that conflicts with evidence from Shroud of Turin

⇒ 3 ⇐

The Greatest
and the Least

And he said to them, "What is it you want me to do for
you?" And they said to him, "Grant us to sit, one at your
right hand and one at you left, in you glory." But Jesus
said to them, "You do not know what you are asking. Are
you able to drink the cup that I drink, or be baptized with
the baptism that I am baptized with?" [MARK 10:36–38]

We are told that there were numerous rabbis in
Israel at the time of Jesus. But he was different
in several ways. First, the other rabbis spent
almost all of their time teaching, explaining, and further
refining the teachings of the Torah—the first five books of
the Scriptures. The stories of the patriarchs, the escape from
Egypt, entry into the holy land, and the Law of Moses were
the bedrock on which Israel was built.

Jesus, of course, honored the traditions and foundations
of his people, but his teachings ranged far and wide—searching and exploring the meaning of God in our lives. His say-
ings were often surprising in their demands ("If your right
hand offend you, cut it off.") and beautiful in their expres-

sion of God's care ("Are not two sparrows sold for a penny? Yet not one of them will fall to the ground outside of your Father's care.").

There are other differences between the traditional rabbis and how Jesus as rabbi worked with his followers. It was the custom for students to select the rabbi they would follow—because they liked his teachings, his person. But Jesus selected disciples to follow him, particularly the Twelve, who were the symbolic core and would help fulfill the destiny of Israel.

Finally, students served their rabbi, bringing meals and assisting with his needs. But Jesus taught and acted as "one who serves." This changed everything and it changed the way his followers, and we, are to treat one another.

Jesus' followers, and perhaps particularly those closest to him, saw his compassion joined to power—over disease and over evil spirits. They witnessed his moral strength dealing with the leaders of Israel. So it was natural that they saw him as one who would restore the nation, drive out the Romans, and reclaim the power they believed God had promised to David and his lineage.

An important part of Jesus' mission was to correct these expectations. In the Gospel of Mark, just before James and John asked to sit at his right and left hand, Jesus, for the third time, predicted his suffering and death. Did they understand his reference to "the baptism that I will be baptized with"? Jesus spoke indirectly, referring to his death, as he always did, as a new beginning, not a disgraceful end. His followers had a great deal of difficulty with this.

How does this apply to us? As he chose his earliest followers, Jesus has selected us. And he expects us to follow by serving one another, by reaching out to those in need, and even by welcoming death as a gift from God.

Also like his earliest followers, we often misunderstand what it means to follow him. Members of the Christian churches have at times considered their calling not as a mission to serve but as a badge of honor, even believing that they, as Christians, were better than others.

For centuries popes lived like princes, with wealth and servants who indeed treated them as lords. Bishops were a step below, but also acting as governors. And priests came to expect not just respect but deference. Now with Pope Francis and his return to the gospels, things are changing.

It is nevertheless for each of us to consider how we might misunderstand what it means to follow Christ. We can gain insight and strength from the example of others.

THE CHRISTIAN EXPERIENCE

In his early years, Ignatius Loyola was a soldier wanting to please his lord and his homeland and win the approval of his woman of the hour. These were common ambitions in late medieval times. He was, however, wounded in battle, his leg badly broken, and he had to spend long months in rehabilitation. He had been accustomed to read romances of chivalry. But at this time the only materials available to him were a life of Christ and a book of lives of the saints. He read them; he pondered what he read; and he paid attention to his feelings. He noticed that contemplating deeds of chivalry left him feeling dry and unsatisfied. But meditating on the message of Christ and the lives of those who followed him made him feel uplifted, with a sense of peace and purpose.

With psychological insights far ahead of his time, Ignatius built from his own experiences a program of meditation and prayer, later called "The Spiritual Exercises." These exercises have led many to a better understanding and appreciation of how God is ready to work in their lives. The exercises quiet the mind, lift the heart, and open the door to the Spirit. You are even now engaging in such exercises.

We do not save ourselves. We are saved by the grace of Christ, the love of God, and the Spirit living within us. For most of us, turning toward God is a lifelong process. St. Ignatius taught that many of the evils we must be on guard against are found in the quest for wealth, pleasure, and power. These three are constantly offered to us in the self-centered generation in which we live—which is still much like other generations.

Greed is everywhere, including within us. It is not easy to root out the acquisitive impulses when popular culture constantly tells us that we must have more—things, money, travel, clothes, and on and on. How we put a stop to this is up to each of us. The first motivation is that we must free ourselves from the lure and the weight of "things" in order to turn our hearts and minds to God. The second motive is that the needs of the poor near us and throughout the world are very great; responding to the needs of others will help us become more connected and free, less isolated, more part of the family of God.

We are also invited to pleasure many times a day. How and why should we deny ourselves? Were we not made for happiness? We were indeed made for happiness, and that is why we should be wary of pleasure. It distracts us from true happiness. In speaking to James and John, Jesus talked about his "baptism": his suffering, his rebirth. Some form of suffering is likely to come our way today, and we will become better followers of Christ if we accept it.

Power is not something that most of us have much of, but the desire to impress our will on others or to be recognized as something special—these impulses are always lurking. We live in a narcissistic age. We want to be noticed and valued for...whatever it might be: our wit, knowledge, or insight. These are not all bad, but they can distract us from the larger good to which Christ our Lord is always trying to lead us.

REFLECTION AND WEEKLY PRACTICE

Saint Ignatius urged his followers, the Jesuits, to examine their consciences twice a day. We might try the same. In what ways have I shown my temper or my desire to look special or smart? How have I neglected those around me? When might a visit or phone call or note have made a difference? In what ways have I cut corners in my work or other responsibilities? There are other questions that only you can ask yourself. We should not become self-absorbed. But we should lead lives close to Christ our Lord. The disciples in the situation we are considering asked Jesus for the wrong thing. We should think carefully about our prayers—what we hope for and pray for.

+ Good insight, nothing objectionable.

⚌ 4 ⚌

To See

"Son of David, have mercy on me!" [MARK 10:48]

"What do you want me to do for you?" [MARK 10:51]

The gospels sometimes seem like a collection of disconnected incidents and teachings. There are, however, central themes and messages. And the order of events can help us better understand what is happening. The exchange we are now considering comes almost immediately after the request of James and John that they have places of honor in Jesus' kingdom. The other disciples became angry at this, and Jesus quietly told them that he came not to be served but to serve, "and to give his life as a ransom for many." This would be the fourth time he mentions his death, in three chapters.

We are told next that they traveled to Jericho, and when they were leaving Jericho in a large crowd, a blind beggar kept calling out. The people tried to hush the man. Jesus stopped and told them to bring the man to him. In an instantaneous turnabout, the people tell the man, Bartimaeus, to take heart, and he asks Jesus to have mercy on him. Jesus asks what he wants.

It would seem clear that the man was blind and knew that

Jesus worked miracles. Why did Jesus ask what he wanted? Jesus interacted with people. We can miss this if we move too quickly to the miracles. Jesus paid attention to people, to their circumstances, their needs and wants. In accordance with this approach, he responded in different ways to different people. In this case the answer was direct and, for us, expected. The man said, "My teacher, let me see again." He uses an intimate form of the word "rabbi." Jesus told the man to go, his faith had saved him. The man received his sight and "followed Jesus on the way." We don't hear about Bartimaeus again, but the Greek name and the mention of "the way" has led commentators to think perhaps he was a member of the early church in that region.

The exchange between Bartimaeus and Jesus naturally makes us think about the importance of prayer, and in particular prayer of petition. For us as believers, asking for God's help, protection, and guidance is as natural as breathing. But we ask ourselves why some prayers seem to be answered and some not. Perhaps this is the wrong question. What we need is prayer that will lead us to the absolute conviction that God is with us, even as God was with Christ—in his suffering and death. Michael Casey explores Jesus' death in a way that we might apply to ourselves.

> Jesus goes to his death not as a hapless victim of malign circumstances but as one who has arrived at the point where he is able to give free assent to the fate that has befallen him as being, in some mysterious way, the expression of his Father's will....His suffering is real, profound, and intense. The only bulwark against utter hopelessness is his certainty of the faithfulness of his Father's love. [MICHAEL CASEY, *FULLY HUMAN, FULLY DIVINE* (LIGOURI/TRIUMPH, 2004)]

So it is with us. We may pray to be relieved from suffering. But we should know with absolute certainty that, whether suffering or not, whether sick or healthy, we are connected to God, sharing in the life of Christ our Lord. Prayer connects us to God and strengthens our life in Christ.

THE CHRISTIAN EXPERIENCE

Mystics and those of deep faith have said that prayer is the most important thing in life. And yet most of us have difficulty squeezing in a few moments here or there. Why is it that the responsibilities of life—family, work, care of home, friends, and even pleasant pastimes—always seem to take priority, claiming our time and energy?

The Way of the Pilgrim is a short book about the importance of prayer. It starts as follows:

By the grace of God I am a Christian man, by my actions a great sinner, and by my calling a homeless wanderer of the humblest birth who roams from place to place. My worldly goods are a knapsack with some dried bread in it on my back, and in my breast pocket a bible. And that is all.

On the twenty-fourth Sunday after Pentecost I went to church to say my prayers here during the liturgy. The first Epistle of St. Paul to the Thessalonians was being read, and among other words I heard these, "Pray without ceasing." It was this text, more than any other, which forced itself upon my mind, and I began to think how it was possible to pray without ceasing, since a man has to concern himself with other things also in order to make a living.

The book recounts the pilgrim's travels, conversations, and prayers, with particular attention to what has become known as the Jesus Prayer: "Lord Jesus Christ, have mercy on me, a sinner."

Returning to Bartimaeus, it is not hard to imagine that he prayed without ceasing. His blindness must have been constantly on his mind. He heard other people talk about all the things they saw—the wonders of nature, the smiles of a friend, the necessities of daily life. And so he wished and prayed that he might see.

How does the request of Bartimaeus, "Lord, that I might see," relate to us? Are there ways in which you and I should pray to "see"? In the natural world, there is a great deal that we do not see. The light and color we see is only a fraction of the full spectrum. We cannot see atoms, electrons, and light waves. But they are everywhere, responsible for much of the physical activities in our lives. Similarly, in the world of faith, there is a great deal that we cannot see.

REFLECTION AND WEEKLY PRACTICE

What does it mean "to see"? We should want to see things and people as Jesus did. We use the word "see" to mean "understand," "appreciate," "value." We try as Christians to see with our hearts as well as our minds. We ask the Holy Spirit to help us understand. Some things may be beyond our understanding, but not if God is with us. Our life of prayer must always be rooted in faith, in the absolute confidence that God is with us individually and in community. This week, Christ our Lord is asking what you want him to do for you. Tell him.

+ - Again, very good. Solid

$\Longrightarrow$ **5** $\Longleftarrow$

A Question

"But who do you say that I am?" Simon Peter answered,
"You are the Messiah, the Son of the living God."

[MATTHEW 16:15–16]

We have all heard that the Eskimos have many words for snow: snow-on-the-ground; falling snow; crusty snow, to name a few. It is natural that there are many names for snow in that frozen world. It is said that they also have many names for reindeer—depending on their temperament, size, and so on. In America, we have a number of words that apply to money: capital, worth, cash, resources, funds, wages, wealth, bucks, bread, dough, etc.

Down through the centuries, those wanting to follow Christ have felt that they themselves were called to answer the question that Jesus asked Peter. And how each of us answers it will determine our response to God, as well as what kind of Christians and people we will be, "Who do you say that I am?" There are indeed many names and titles for Christ, and indeed for God. But I think to some extent we have lost touch with them.

And this is part of the problem: the question has been

asked and answered so often that we might find it shopworn and no longer relevant. Rainer Maria Rilke asks,

> Who is this Christ that is meddling in everything? He did not know anything about us, about our work, about our misery, about our joys and the ways in which we work, suffer, and summon joy, yet who seemingly and persistently demands of us to make him first in our lives.

In fact, for hundreds of years before Christ and these two thousand years since he walked the earth, prophets and saints, missionaries and sinners have struggled to find the words. Have we perhaps lost interest, lost the excitement in applying different words to God, to the Messiah.

OLD TESTAMENT PREVIEW

In the Book of Isaiah we find more than fifty names and models for God and about a dozen names for the Messiah. These are helpful because we have to work to give meaning to the words "God," and "Christ," which means Messiah, the Anointed One.

Consider the title "Wonderful Counselor." Do we ever think of God, of Jesus, as counselor? We need counseling, guidance, direction. And if we are attentive, the Spirit of God will indeed guide us.

In chapter 7, Isaiah talks about Immanuel, God with us. In this case he proclaims not about the God who created, led the people out of Egypt, and spoke through Moses, but rather about one who would be born of woman and, in our view, would be God with his people. This is indeed what Jesus means to us. He is God among us, or as Jesus said, "the kingdom of God is among you."

Further on in Isaiah chapter 53, the prophet talks about the servant who will suffer for our transgressions and carry the iniquity of us all. These passages perhaps more than any other in all of Scripture stir our hearts to appreciate what Christ means as redeemer. And we know that we will also have to suffer. But again, God will be with us, individually and in community.

In chapter 61, Isaiah speaks of a messenger, whom the Lord has sent.

> The Spirit of the Lord God is upon me, because the Lord has anointed me; he has sent me to bring good news to the oppressed, to bind up the brokenhearted and release the prisoners. [ISAIAH 61:1]

Jesus appropriated these words to himself: In Luke's gospel, he reads these words and then announces that the prophecy has been fulfilled.

In the Book of Deuteronomy, God tells Moses about a special prophet that God will raise up, "a prophet like you," who will speak to the people. For Christians, this rather obscure prophet is Jesus, who in many ways represents, particularly in Mathew's gospel, a second Moses: one who leads his people to new understandings, to a new relationship with God, in a new covenant.

In his book *Jesus through the Centuries*, Jaroslav Pelikan describes how thinking about Jesus has adapted to the needs and concerns of different times and peoples. Jesus has been viewed, honored, and imitated as an itinerant rabbi, teaching and awakening people to the mysteries of God's kingdom, and a light to the Gentiles, fulfilling the hopes and prophecies, particularly of the Greek and Roman world who believed in the spiritual dimensions of human existence. In later centuries, the monks related to Jesus as a man of prayer, one with the Father. And so it has been down through the centuries. In our own day, Jesus has been viewed as a social reformer, bringing hope to the poor and even encouraging the rearrangement of social structures that have oppressed so many.

REFLECTION

Jesus asks each of us, "Who do you say that I am?" There are many answers; it is up to each of us to decide where we stand and who Jesus is in our lives. One of the traditional answers is that Christ is priest, prophet, and king—traditional, but we can make it new in our minds and hearts. A priest is one who offers sacrifice. In the New Testament, Jesus offers himself; he is the high priest. Perhaps we, as Catholics, have lost some of the power of Christ as high priest in using the title "priest" for our clergy. But more recently the church has reemphasized the expression "priestly people." We, as a people, all share with our Lord in the offering of sacrifice.

A prophet is one who speaks out. Jesus spoke fearlessly in favor of the poor and powerless and condemned those who tried to enforce rules that did not move people toward God.

And how do we relate to "king"? Does Christ as king speak to us? Perhaps we spend too much time and invest too much in our political allegiances. How bound should Christianity be with any particular government or political process? How do your politics relate to Christ? Our allegiance to Christ as king of our lives should be absolute.

WEEKLY PRACTICE

Write down who Jesus is for you, in your life, in your personal relationships. How does Jesus meddle in your life, trying to get your attention and your love and service?

 + Good

$\Longrightarrow$ **6** $\Longleftarrow$

Try Something Different

Jesus said to them, "Children, you have no fish, have you?" They answered him, "No." He said to them, "Cast the net to the right side of the boat, and you will find some." [JOHN 21:5-6]

These verses are part of the resurrection stories in John's gospel. The first word of Jesus, "Children," reminds us that translation always implies some interpretation, and the interpretation guides our reading. In this case, various translations of Jesus calling to the disciples use the words children or friends or fellows or lads—each of which has a different ring to our ear. So interpretation is required, and these reflections encourage you to better understand the meaning of Scripture in the light of your life and experiences—to interpret for yourself. The word "children," of course, implies familiarity as well as love and care—both of which Jesus had cultivated throughout the years with his disciples. Still, it is not quite what we would expect a workingman to say to his friends. "Guys?" This would be a bit too familiar.

The narrative goes on to say that the disciples at first did not recognize Jesus. Then they did what he suggested and caught a very large number of fish. They went ashore and found that Jesus was preparing a meal for them.

It is conjectured that this incident was adapted from the Gospel of Luke in which a very similar episode takes place early in the narrative. Perhaps the author of the fourth gos- *Modern* *ish* pel wanted to stress that the post-resurrection community around Jesus was a continuation of discipleship but also the start of something new. Jesus gives the community and his disciples support and guidance as they begin their work without him. It is important to remember that each of the gospels has the stamp of an individual in its style, emphasis, and goals. But the later authors borrowed freely from what was available to them. The gospels were written in community and we should read them in community. *No evidence of this*

The story draws us in as Jesus redirects the fishing. Did he have special, even supernatural knowledge of the location of the fish? Did he put them there? Some have seen it that way. It has also been said that the right side was the lucky side for fishing or that someone from shore might have been able to see a school of fish that could not be seen from the boat.

Perhaps Jesus was suggesting that the disciples try something different, and the Holy Spirit has suggested the same to Christians through the ages. But the institutional church has often resisted "something different."

Because the church was heir not only to the teachings and example of Jesus but also to Roman laws and Greek philosophy, Christianity adopted legal and philosophical approaches that sometimes seemed at odds with the spirit of the gospels. And in time corrections were needed.

The church wanted to protect "the sacred mysteries." The Latin language was retained for the liturgy even as the ethnic groups of Europe converting to Christianity did not understand it. The Mass moved further from the people, becoming the property of the priest, and seemed to be a spectacle rather than communal prayer; it was certainly not a meal.

THE CHRISTIAN EXPERIENCE

Scripture also became the property of "the teaching church." The hierarchy was afraid that the people reading Scripture on their own would not get it right and might be led astray. So reading the Bible was discouraged. John Wycliffe, in the fourteenth century, sometimes called the morning star of the Reformation, was censured for translating the Bible into English.

Then came Martin Luther. He and Johannes Gutenberg changed everything. Luther's translation of the Bible into German (widely disseminated by Gutenberg's printing presses) and his approach to the liturgy brought the Christian message closer to the people. As a Catholic I was brought up to see Luther as a heretic who tried to destroy the church. Then came Vatican II, and we as Catholics accepted much of what Luther had taught and practiced. We tried something different but not really new, and we are finding Christ in our midst—in Scripture, in prayer, and in community.

Most recently we are discovering that we must try something different with regard to women in the church. They have been almost completely left out of the consultations and decision making in the Catholic Church. They are refused membership in the priesthood and hierarchy. It has been said that this is like breathing with one lung or thinking with half a brain.

The book *Catholic Women Speak: Bringing Our Gifts to the Table* lives up to its title. In brief, clearly written essays, the women speak about every aspect of the church and women: their important work in some parish ministries; liturgy; conscience and contraception; women on the margins; women not preaching and not participating in synods. One contributor writes about her experiences:

> I have been privileged to come alongside parishioners navigating situations including crisis pregnancies, domestic violence, medical emergencies, detention and deportation of family members.

In every area of life we recognize that women have special talents and gifts; we try to develop teams that include both men and women, knowing that such teams will be stronger and more effective. Also, in the church we are learning that community is diminished and weakened when women do not play active roles.

As in the practices that the Reformation brought forward that were later validated and accepted by the Catholic Church—the importance of Scripture, the use of the vernacular, and an emphasis on faith—so in recent years some Protestant churches have ordained women and accepted their importance at all levels of decision making. In our town the pastor of the Congregational Church was raised as a Catholic. She felt called to service and ministry. But she told me that while kneeling near the front of the church at the first Mass of a priest, she "heard" a voice say, "You are not welcome here." I don't know further details of her spiritual journey, but she studied theology, entered the ministry, and has served as an inspiring pastor.

Returning to the book mentioned above, we read an indictment of the Catholic position. What is the impact on the family of a church where Sunday after Sunday only men preach? How does it affect the family to be told that only men can be the *imago Christi*, "the image of Christ"? And what is it like to have all the decisions at the upper levels of the church made by men? Men have been systematically privileged in the Catholic Church, and women systematically discriminated against. Let's hope the time is coming to try something different.

REFLECTION

Regarding Jesus' advice to "cast your nets on the other side," perhaps each of us needs to look at our own lives of faith. Change is not easy. But Jesus may be calling on you and me to make a change. Change takes place in different areas of life. Through learning and experience and experimentation, science makes progress. When taking a trip that we have carefully planned, we sometimes find that the unanticipated detours are richly rewarding. In meeting new people, we may find unexpected friends. Christ our Lord is calling to us, and sometimes he is telling us to try something different.

WEEKLY PRACTICE

Write a list of things in the church or Christian community that you think should be different. For each, write how you, in some small way, might be able to help make things different.

– Undoes all the good that goes before. Ignores the results of the change he advocates

7

The Things That Are Caesar's

But knowing their hypocrisy, he said to them, "Why are you putting me to the test? Bring me a denarius and let me see it." And they brought one. Then he said to them, "Whose head is this, and whose title?" They answered, "The emperor's." Jesus said to them, "Give to the emperor the things that are the emperor's, and to God the things that are God's." And they were utterly amazed at him. [MARK 12:15–17]

From the dawn of nations and governments, through the times of Egyptian, Greek, Roman, and other empires, or even tribes and small ethnic groups, gods and spirits have played important roles in public affairs. Roman emperors were sometimes declared divine after their deaths, or even while still living.

For the people of Israel, God was a central fact—in history and in government, in peace and in war, for the individual and for the nation. As a result, the Roman occupiers, at the time of Christ, were seen as violating God's plan. Their overthrow and the restoration of the nation were expected and

33

anticipated. It was therefore easy to set a trap for Jesus. If he said it was right to pay taxes, he could be seen as a collaborator rather than a prophet sent by God. If he spoke against taxes, he could be handed over to the Romans as a traitor. The Roman rule did not require a great deal from the nations that were occupied, but taxes were essential.

In answering the question, Jesus took a middle road, separating God from the state. His maxim has echoed through the centuries, although nations and ethnic groups have sometimes wanted to identify the church with themselves. At times the Catholic Church taught that heretical teaching should not be permitted and that the state should suppress such teachings and practices. Protestant traditions have taken similar paths.

The framers of the U.S. Constitution inserted a very powerful amendment, linking the exercise of religion with several other freedoms.

> Congress shall make no law respecting an establishment of religion, or prohibiting the free exercise thereof; or abridging the freedom of speech, or of the press; or the right of the people peaceably to assemble, and to petition the government for a redress of grievances.

Interactions between church and state have been complex. The church must be vigilant not to be co-opted into supporting whatever the government wishes. We have seen in recent history how fascism required and obtained support from Christian churches. *True, but we have also seen brave opposition leading to martydom: St. Maximilian Kolbe*

THE CHRISTIAN EXPERIENCE

Where does the church stand with regard to violence and war, particularly when it is a policy of the state? I'm not sure. There have been pacifists, like Dorothy Day, who were against all war, plain and simple. But what does the teaching church tell us? In a letter of May 11, 2015, the U.S. Conference of Catholic Bishops wrote to the U.N. about the use of drones.

> Armed drones may be used outside of areas of open and protracted fighting if it is determined that the person targeted poses an imminent threat, if the use of lethal force is proportionate and there is no other means to prevent the threat to life (i.e. "last resort"), and if civilian casualties can be avoided as much as possible.

The tone is more legalistic than gospel. "Just war" has been discussed through the centuries. The idea is to limit violence, killing, and the ravages of war. But the underlying message, as in the statement above, seems to be that we are stuck with war, and the best we can do is try to circumscribe the violence and the damage incurred in rendering to Caesar.

The bishops have also made numerous pronouncements on abortion. The following is from "Living the Gospel of Life," 1998. It is not about those directly involved in abortion but about "Catholic officials" who do not take action against abortion.

> Those who justify their inaction on the grounds that abortion is the law of the land need to recognize that there is a higher law, the law of God. No human law can validly contradict the Commandment: "Thou shalt not kill."

The statement does not try to circumscribe a necessary evil, as with drones, but warns of sin. The reasoning is that abortion is the direct killing of innocent life, whereas in the use of drones, civilian casualties are to be avoided "as much as possible."

Perhaps linking the discussion of war with abortion would challenge us. Suppose the bishops were to say, "We judge that belonging to the American armed forces is an evil of the same magnitude as participating in an abortion." Many Catholics would say that is ridiculous. We need armed forces to protect us. And soldiers do not kill without "imminent threat." But shouldn't Christians take a stand, especially if they are citizens of one of the most militaristic nations on earth? Military events are not in fact easily circumscribed. We are all complicit in the violence of war: in paying taxes, owning stock in weapons-producing companies, and in failing to question the policies that support killing. We are complicit in abortion in similar ways. We should consider our involvement in promoting a violent and war-like nation.

It has been reported that Pope Francis wants to review and revise the just war theory. For the time being, he said in a homily, "Jesus is weeping today, too, because we have preferred the path of war, the path of hatred, the path of enmity." When we have doubts about the centrality of nonviolence in Christ's message, we have only to look at the cross. "He was led like a lamb to the slaughter."

REFLECTION

In today's world Christians have to be very careful not to link our faith with politics. The goals and activities of governments and political parties are never the same as the mission of the church. Their leaders have often tried, sometimes successfully, to co-opt Christians into their ranks. While we Christians should participate in public life, we must be wary of the ways in which political leaders try to use Christian principles simply to further their own efforts toward power, greed, and a host of unjust practices. Our sense of self-worth should come only from belonging to Christ.

WEEKLY PRACTICE

Talk with your spouse or a good friend about how your political activities and thoughts might be in conflict with your beliefs and life as a Christian.

- Another bad chapter -
doesn't try to clarify.
Takes too much liberty
with the Gospel cited.

8

Two Blind Men

As Jesus went on from there, two blind men followed
him, crying loudly, "Have mercy on us, Son of David!"
When he entered the house, the blind men came to him;
and Jesus said to them. "Do you believe that I am able
to do this?" They said to him, "Yes, Lord." Then he
touched their eyes and said, "According to your faith let
it be done to you." [MATTHEW 9:27-29]

As in the other encounters we are considering, every word here is telling. Earlier in Matthew's gospel we read that he "made his home in Capernaum." In this case, it appears that he was indeed on his way home. The blind men are following, perhaps with friends leading them or perhaps just staying near the noise and excitement of the crowd. Jesus apparently does not pay much attention to them. But when he gets home, he does not close the door on them. They take this as a silent invitation, and they follow him in.

Then the encounter begins. "Do you believe?" he asks. They say they do. Who wouldn't? It might mean gaining or regaining sight. Then comes the clincher, Jesus says that seeing depends on their faith. They are partners in the healing.

Jesus finds us where we are, as we are. And we respond to his invitation in our own way.

THE CHRISTIAN EXPERIENCE

The saints provide lessons for us about how God meets people "where they are." And as he did with blind men, Jesus helps us to see more clearly.

St. Thomas More was born in 1478, the son of a lawyer in England. He became a lawyer, married and had four children, and became an advisor to King Henry VIII. There was a charm and simplicity to More's life, even as he became lord chancellor, one of the most powerful positions in the country.

These were turbulent times. Henry VIII divorced his wife Catherine and wanted an annulment from the pope so that he could marry again and produce a male heir. When the pope refused, Henry left the Catholic Church and took England with him. He formed the Church of England, with himself as head. All of the leading men in the church and government had to swear an oath recognizing the king as head of the church. When More said he could not take the oath, he was arrested for high treason.

Playwright Robert Bolt captures well More's spirit in his famous play *A Man for All Seasons*. At one point in the play, during More's trial, a friend and leading statesmen asks, perhaps in good faith, if More could not join them, endorsing the king, "for old times' sake." More, however, sees things differently. He answers, "And when you are ushered into eternal happiness for following your conscience, and I am sent to eternal damnation for not following mine, will you join me for old times' sake?"

He is worth considering in connection with seeing because with the eyes of faith More saw the important things with great clarity. He composed a beautiful prayer for "good humor," which might be the equivalent of a "sense of humor," in our vernacular.

Grant me, O Lord, good digestion, and also something to
　digest.
Grant me a healthy body, and the necessary good humor to
　maintain it.
Grant me a simple soul that knows to treasure all that is good
　and that doesn't frighten easily at the sight of evil,
　　but rather finds the means to put things back in their place.
Give me a soul that knows not boredom, grumblings, sighs
　and laments,
nor excess of stress, because of that obstructing thing
　called "I."
Grant me, O Lord, a sense of good humor.
Allow me the grace to be able to take a joke to discover in life
　a bit of joy,
and to be able to share it with others.

REFLECTION

The two blind men appealing to Jesus and St. Thomas More
were different in many ways. But they had faith—the blind
men, that Jesus could cure them, and More that he must
follow his conscience. We ought to pray frequently for the
faith we will need—in whatever circumstances of life we find
ourselves.

A conscience informed by the Church

WEEKLY PRACTICE

Jesus once admonished his followers that we should not be
so critical of others, "taking the speck out of another's eye"
while there is a log in our own. This is a rather grotesque met-
aphor. But isn't it true that we have great difficulty seeing our
own faults? This week, pray for God's help to understand and
"see" who you are—with all your faults and sins. The better
we know ourselves, the more we will be able to help those
around us.

— He fails to point out that More's conscience was informed by the Church. Henry VIII also acted out of conscience — with devastating results.

= 9 =

God and Nature

He said to them, "Where is your faith?" They were
afraid and amazed, and said to one another, "Who then
is this, that he commands even the winds and the water,
and they obey him?" [LUKE 8:25]

N ature, the world in which we live, presents itself in
more ways than we can count. The world around
us is beautiful, fascinating, sometimes terrifying,
and much more. The people of Israel believed that all creation
was good and that God's rule was total. After Job's many mis-
fortunes, God ridicules him, pointing out how little he knows
of the mysteries in the world around him. First, God talks
about the land animals and how wonderfully they do what
they were made for. Then God talks about Leviathan, and the
images of this giant of the sea continue for a full chapter.

> When it raises itself up the gods are afraid;
> at the crashing they are beside themselves.
> [JOB 41:25]

The psalms also celebrate the wonders of God's world, on the
land and in the sea.

O Lord, how manifold are your works!
In wisdom you have made them all;
the earth is full of your creatures.
Yonder is the sea, great and wide,
creeping things innumerable are there,
living things both small and great.

[**PSALM** 104:24–25]

We, like the Israelites of old, marvel at the power and beauty of nature. But it is different for us. Humans have conquered the whales, and yet we continue to learn more about the beauty of their communications, their care for their young, and their migrations. Science tells us a great deal about nature, weather, storms, and destruction. We tend not to place all our concerns before God. We have conquered nature, or so we think. And yet we abuse nature at our peril.

But still we wonder. As I write this, we have heard about an earthquake in Italy that has taken more than three hundred lives. What was God's role in this? What sorts of prayers should we offer? How should we respond when threatened by natural disasters?

THE CHRISTIAN EXPERIENCE

The word "respond," of course, makes us think of "first responders," those who are the first to arrive—to put out the fire, to provide medical care, to rebuild. Pope Francis has said that the church should see itself as a field hospital. We then should see ourselves as working in that hospital—attending to those in need. Most first responders' work is finished when the fire is out or the injured have been treated and transported to hospitals. Our work as Christians may be just beginning at that time. It is for us, by our words of encouragement and our example, to point toward the God who cares for us all.

This brings us back to the destruction caused by "nature." What are we to think? Is it God's will that such things occur?

This question has been asked for centuries. Perhaps it is the wrong question. We live in a world that is open to our understanding but constantly revealing itself as beyond us. Our world demands constant investigation and re-investigation. And the central fact is that science, like every other human enterprise, has advanced in community. Each scientist adds to the structure of understanding. Consider any little corner of science, calculating temperature and what it means, for example. It seems so simple, and yet it requires some understanding of heat and cold and how they affect the world around us; developing ways to measure, such as the mercury thermometer with its scale; an understanding of how temperatures are related to freezing and melting; and on and on, until today "we" are able to approximate the global temperature from year to year and to talk about global warming. How many people have been involved in this process? Let's say thousands, going back centuries. We are community and in fact have functioned rather well as community.

But we do not understand enough or appreciate how much we belong to and are a part of one another. Yes, some of us die young, and some live long lives. Some live in squalor and some live in ease. But we are all connected. The cells of our bodies are continually dying and renewing themselves. So it is for humanity and for the body of Christ. We have different roles to play. But we share life. Who is to say that living a long life is better than living a short life? Christ our Lord was killed in the prime of life. But we consider his to have been the perfect life. It is difficult for us to accept the fact that what we do continues, even here on earth, after we die. St. Thérèse of Lisieux died young, saying she would spend her heaven doing good on earth. This can be true for each of us.

Was it wrong for the disciples, in the midst of the storm, to cry to Jesus for help? Not at all. But we do not in fact know what is best for us. St. Ignatius included among the rules for Jesuits "that they should thank God for sickness seeing it is no less a gift than health." Perhaps we could say also, "They should thank God for storms seeing they are no less a gift than fair weather."

REFLECTION

Whether we are in a beautiful sunny day or a dark and stormy night, we are in God's world. It is the God who is infinitely beyond our imaginings and deeply within our every breath. But still we are not comfortable with a God who defies the laws of nature. The disciples said, as we would, "Who then is this that he commands even the winds and the water, and they obey him?" Who indeed is this Christ Jesus? We must ask ourselves this question each day. He is connected to God; he brought God among us. We must turn to him in every storm, as a people. We are bound together; we belong to one another. Every prayer we say should be to better connect us to God in Jesus Christ—and to one another.

WEEKLY PRACTICE

Spend some time each day considering how you are connected with the world of nature. Meditate on the changing seasons, the wonder of the sun with the light and warmth that come to us, the loveliness of fruits and vegetables and flowers. Consider how you and those around you are part of the world of nature. Consider how you work with God to maintain this great world, the work of God.

— He fails to acknowledge that
we live in a fallen world,
with predictible results of
humanism & modernism.

PART II

JESUS RESPONDS

We often think that spontaneous comments or responses are spoken without thought or preparation. Sometimes that is the case. But I think in the life of Jesus it was different. When he answers quickly and briefly, spontaneously, it seems that his comments arise not off the top of his head but from the depths of his soul.

It is clear that Jesus spent a great deal of time contemplating the kingdom—it was his mission, the enterprise on which his life was based. This kingdom took hold of his prayer life, his imagination, and his teaching. And so it was perfectly natural that when someone suggested that his mother is blessed, he would respond by saying that those who accept the word of God, the kingdom, are blessed.

We should try to develop an attachment to God's way of doing things, to the way Jesus thinks—so that our spontaneous, unreflective responses will be about the kingdom, the message, and the promises of Christ, our Lord.

As it
He didn't
know the
will
God?

⇒ **10** ⇐

To Hear
the Word
of God

"Blessed is the womb that bore you, and the breasts that nursed you." But he said, "Rather: blessed are those who hear the word of God and keep it." [LUKE 11:27-28]

This is one of the many examples of Jesus listening and responding to someone he does not know. We might start by imagining what the woman was feeling and thinking. She had been following Jesus. She was overcome with excitement at what she heard. He talked about how God is like an earthly father but more attentive and concerned. Jesus healed those afflicted by diseases of the body, mind, and spirit; he spoke with compassion about God's love and mercy. He said that in God's love the hairs of your head are numbered. The woman was overwhelmed with excitement.

The woman's blessing of Jesus' mother was in fact directed toward Jesus himself, as we might say of someone, "He must have had a wonderful upbringing," or "I wish I had known his parents." We know well that early nourishing, physical and emotional, is important. So it was that the woman could not contain her enthusiasm. She called out in wonder at this person who was changing everything.

And Jesus called out to her. What he said is sometimes taken to be a correction of the woman's comment. Perhaps; but we can also think of his remark as a clarification, asking her to think in a different direction: "Yes, my mother was blessed by God; and I am blessed. But the more important thing is for each of you to listen to the word of God." And we pray that we might listen to the word of God the way his mother did. Jesus is returning the blessing to this woman, as one who has heard and listened to the word of God.

And might this brief encounter have helped Jesus better understand his ministry? He was fully human and like us striving to better know who he was, his world, his work, and those around him. He had grown up and matured, learning about and experiencing the history of his people and their connections to God. In many encounters, he gently—or sometimes not so gently—redirects a person's thinking. Israel had been oppressed for several centuries, and people wanted to throw off the occupiers who usurped their land and traditions. Jesus was telling them that God's love was now calling them to renewal, but in a different way.

Jesus' followers were of course familiar with the word of God. And "hearing the word of God" was not new to them. Creation itself took place through God's word, "And God said…" In Scripture the proclamations of the prophets often began with the expression, "The word of the Lord came to…." The prophets spoke with conviction and urgency about God's message. The Law itself was handed down in words. So Jesus embeds his work and his mission in the teachings of his people. He calls those who wish to follow to a completeness of life in God, not a break from those who came before him. The people of Israel were approaching a critical point in their existence. Jesus tells them to listen, to pay close attention to what came before and to what is happening in the present moment. He, Jesus, the Word of God, is in their midst.

And what does it mean for us—to hear and keep the word of God?

The Scriptures are indeed rich in wisdom and guidance. Your reflections right now are letting the word of God enter more deeply into your mind and heart and soul. Sometimes the word of God comes to us quietly like a gentle rain—and sometimes more like a violent storm.

OLD TESTAMENT PREVIEW

Consider the prophet Nathan when he went to see David. David had sinned, taking Bathsheba to himself and giving orders that her husband, Uriah, should be isolated in battle, deliberately left alone by those around him, to be killed by the enemy soldiers.

After Uriah was killed in battle, Nathan came to David and told him a story. There was a rich man who had many cattle and sheep and a great farm. And on his land lived a poor man with his family. The poor man had only one little ewe lamb; it was a pet, sharing his food, and "it even slept in his arms." A traveler came to visit the rich man, and instead of giving one of his many sheep to feed the traveler, the rich man took the poor man's lamb, killed it, and fed his guest. When David heard this he became very angry and said that the rich man should be punished for what he had done.

And Nathan the prophet said to David, "You are the man." The story is a parable and David got the point. He repented his sin, and God forgave him. Is there something in the story for us? Do we in some ways take from those who have little in order to satisfy ourselves? How ought we repent and redirect our lives? The words of Scripture challenge us.

This is what it means to hear the word of God and keep it.

We hear the word of God explored and explained in reflections, and so it has been down through the ages. You and I have been in the mind and plans of God from eternity. Is this possible? That God treasures, values, and loves billions of people? Why not? God has enough love and goodness for all of us. It is for us to recognize and accept God's love—in one another and in ourselves. We are not alone; we are part of the great human family. We are connected to God and to one another.

Let us return our reflection to the woman. "Blessed," she said. What do we mean when we say that we have or some other person has been blessed? Usually we are talking about health or good jobs or perhaps happy, successful children. This is a notion that runs through parts of the Old Testament. God blesses Abraham with a family, a people, and land—after much waiting. So it is with others: a long life, a family, and other good things—these are signs of God's favor.

Or are they?

Jesus looked at life very differently. "Blessed are you who are poor. For yours is the kingdom of God," he said. We look for a hundred ways to explain that this does not mean quite what it says. But a few verses later, Jesus says, "Woe to you who are rich." He wants us to get the point.

When Jesus said, "Blessed are those who hear the word of God and keep it," he didn't mean that they would have a long and prosperous life. We must ask the Spirit to come into our minds and hearts and help us understand what Jesus says in the gospels and also within our minds and hearts.

REFLECTION AND WEEKLY PRACTICE

Are you a good listener? The question sounds a bit corny, perhaps overworked. But it will happen today and tomorrow that someone will talk to you in ways that show they are searching for God, striving to better connect themselves with that mystery within each of us. Listen closely; you can help others find God within and beyond their lives. Listen and you will find God in your own heart and soul. We are all meant for something more than this world. We can help one another find that something—in the love and teachings of Jesus Christ—if we listen.

⇒ 11 ⇐

John the Baptizer

John would have prevented him, saying, "I need to be baptized by you, and do you come to me?" But Jesus answered him, "Let it be so now; for it is proper for us in this way to fulfill all righteousness."

[MATTHEW 3:14-15]

John the Baptist (or Baptizer) is important in the gospels, and beyond. He is viewed as the last of the prophets and the starting point for Jesus and his followers. The prophets are central in the history of Israel and in the unfolding of God's plan for his people. In Scripture, God speaks to the prophets and the prophets speak to the people on behalf of God.

> Listen to me, O coastlands,
> pay attention, you peoples from far away!
> The Lord called me before I was born,
> while I was in my mother's womb he named me.
>
> [ISAIAH 49:1]

We might consider not only John the Baptist but also ourselves to be the "peoples from far away" that the prophet calls to across the seas and down through the centuries. The word of God still comes to us. God's presence, his word, is within each of us.

Isaiah chapter 40 begins with a message of comfort: "Speak tenderly to Jerusalem." And the verses go on, "prepare the way of the LORD," verses quoted by Matthew and applied to John. The message continues, telling about God's loving care for all those in the world and the futility of worshiping things made by human beings. This is one of the most wonderful chapters in the Old Testament, with so much for us to meditate on: that we are all in God's hands, that God is so far beyond our understanding, and yet that God is close to us.

The worship of idols, forbidden by the first commandment and condemned by the prophets, is something we generally consider outdated. We are not tempted to worship material things made by human hands. Or are we? Consider the advertisements on TV and in magazines; consider yourself as you buy clothes or a car. Don't we too often place our hope and our trust in the things we buy, in the way we look? It has always been so. We alter the way we look, the way we appear to others, even the way we smell—in order to be more acceptable.

John the Baptist went strongly against the current of living well, looking good, and trusting the popular cultural currents of the day. We are told that he wore an animal skin and ate insects and wild honey. He wanted to strip down, showing that his life was rooted in God alone. Because of the simplicity of his life, people were attracted to him, Jesus among them.

Some have suggested that Jesus was one of John's disciples for months, perhaps even a few years. We cannot say, but we should not be scandalized by the idea; nor should we think that this would diminish Jesus and his connection to the Father. Jesus was thoroughly human. He learned as we do, from others. He experienced the joy and excitement that come from understanding. Most of all he grew in understanding God's life in his own life and in the lives of those around him. We can be sure that he meditated on and learned from the prophets.

OLD TESTAMENT PREVIEW

The responsorial psalm for the feast of John's nativity is taken from Psalm 139 and includes.

> For it was you who formed my inward parts;
> you knit me together in my mother's womb.
> I praise you, for I am fearfully and wonderfully made.
> Wonderful are your works. [PSALM 139:13-14]

It almost takes our breath away to contemplate how the psalmist sees not only the wonderful works of God, as we read in many psalms, but also includes himself as being created and known by God. Thus creation and prophecy are linked in some mysterious way.

The Jewish tradition made use of washings as rituals; they were rituals of renewal. The submersion of John's baptism was a mini death, followed by new life. So John agreed; he baptized Jesus. And Jesus followed John, listening and learning. Although John demanded much of himself, leading a hard life, he was gentle and reasonable with those asking his advice. John told the soldiers to be satisfied with their pay and the tax collectors not to collect more than was just; he told those with two tunics to give one to the person who had none.

In his own thinking and in his actions, John was preparing to introduce Jesus. Introductions are important. The introduction generally includes a few words in which the two people are told of common interests or other connections that will give them a start in conversation. Sometimes these casual conversations lead to friendships or shared projects.

John introduced Jesus, not with a few flattering words, but with an announcement that something big is about to happen.

> "I baptize you with water for repentance, but one who is more powerful than I is coming after me; I am not worthy to carry his sandals. He will baptize you with the Holy Spirit and fire."
>
> [**MATTHEW 3:11**]

This is perhaps a little like the introduction that an artist or a scientist might make with a pupil: "I have taught you as much as I can and have taken you as far as I can. But this new mentor is much more accomplished than I and will take you to new levels." Of course, the message in John is much more than that. What did this mean: "he will baptize with the Holy Spirit and fire"?

In the Acts of the Apostles we read that the person selected to take the place of Judas should be one who was among them, "beginning from the baptism of John until the day when he was taken up from us—one of these must become a witness with us to his resurrection."

It was that community of witnesses that became the core of Jesus' followers. At Pentecost they were indeed baptized with the Holy Spirit and fire. So in the story of John the Baptist we are given a preamble to the mystery of Jesus and his first followers.

We know that John was killed in a way that seems almost trivial. Salome dances; her father promises anything; she asks for John's head; he gives it. We accept this as part of God's plan. But what about our own lives? When someone dies in a seemingly random and meaningless way, what does it mean? We can only say that we are bound together, as one people. Baptism connects us to Christ our Lord and to one another. That unbreakable bond transcends and gives meaning to the seemingly meaningless events of our daily lives. When one close to us, or even far away, dies, something in us also dies. And that is the law of life, reminding us that we will indeed die.

REFLECTION

And why did Jesus insist on his baptism by John? Because he wanted to make it clear that he is one of us—not a sinner but part of our sinful situation. He is one of us, bound to us in being human and also in belonging to God. When we join our lives to Christ our Lord we are bound to God and to one another.

WEEKLY PRACTICE

We can also imitate John in introducing others to Jesus: "Would you like to join me at our church? I pray for you often." And most of all we can introduce others to Christ our Lord in our service and response in times of need. Jesus sees our service as being done for him. Try this week in whatever way you can to bring another person to Christ.

12

Dinner
at Levi's

When the scribes of the Pharisees saw that he was eating with sinners and tax collectors, they said to his disciples, "Why does he eat with tax collectors and sinners?" When Jesus heard this, he said to them, "Those who are well have no need of a physician, but those who are sick; I have come to call not the righteous but sinners." [MARK 2:16–17]

This exchange comes after Levi had been called from his work as a tax collector to follow Jesus. There are three paintings by Caravaggio in the church San Luigi dei Francesi in Rome. They depict three events in the life of Levi, who became Matthew. The first and most famous created a stir when it was first shown. The reason is that the figures are clothed as people were at Caravaggio's time, not as was usually done, imagining the clothing of New Testament times. The setting is what might be the backroom of a tavern. Several of the men are gathered around a table apparently counting money. Off to the right, we see Jesus pointing to Matthew, who is seated among friends, perhaps fellow bankers. Matthew points to himself seeming to ask, "Me?" His other hand is near the money. He has not yet made up his mind.

Works of art and literature can help us better understand the human condition, the struggles of mind and heart that all of us endure. Reflecting on this artwork can help us gain insight into Jesus, his mission, and how he dealt with those around him. You can find a reproduction of the painting, "The Calling of St. Matthew," online.

We know from the gospel stories that Matthew did accept Jesus' invitation, followed him, and became one of the Twelve. But he was indeed a tax collector. I live in a small town, and we have a tax collector. She is a kindly woman, known to most of us. She sends out notices when taxes are due; accepts the checks, by mail or in person, and keeps the books; and I suppose sends notices to those who are late. We are of course all aware of the IRS, which for most of us, most of the time, is a faceless organization that collects taxes, develops rules, and follows up on them.

It was different in Jesus' time. Roman rule varied based on the provinces and traditions of the people they had conquered. Rome often let nations and people follow local customs, maintaining their beliefs and religious practices. But the Romans did not like anything that smelled of insurrection or rebellion, and they required taxes. It seems they didn't care very much how the tax collectors operated, as long there was enough to support the troops and send provisions and booty back to Rome.

So Matthew's business was, in modern terms, perhaps more like a collection agency. The tax collectors may have extorted money, taken bribes, and been greedy. But Jesus saw something else. The gospels don't tell us what might have that attracted Jesus to Matthew, but he called and Matthew answered.

And Matthew wanted to celebrate the new direction his life had taken. He threw a party, a dinner party we might say. He invited those with whom he worked, as well as other acquaintances; some of them were religious leaders.

The customs surrounding eating were important to the Jews. There were washings and special utensils and other customs that the "righteous" observed. The common folks often did not maintain all of these practices. So the scribes asked why Jesus ate with sinners.

THE CHRISTIAN EXPERIENCE

Now I would ask you to think back to the verses at the start of this section. Jesus said he came to (*blank*) sinners. What is the missing word, the verb? Many words are used in the Scriptures and in tradition to describe Jesus' mission: to save, redeem, justify, forgive; and I am sure you can think of others. But what Jesus said at that dinner party was that he came "to *call* sinners."

Through the centuries, the church has often used the word "call" to refer to those who entered some special ministry. Sin is generally considered something to avoid, confess, run from. But others have suggested that, being human, our tendencies toward evil and our desire to do good may be intertwined. In one of his earliest interviews, Pope Francis when asked who he was said simply, "a sinner." What a wonderful thought! You and I are sinners, and because we are sinners, Jesus calls us.

But, also in the verses we are considering, Jesus said that

those who are ill need a physician, not those who are well. Doctors examine our bodies, consider the symptoms, and prescribe remedies. These remedies might be medicines; they might also be better diet and exercise. So it is in the world of the spirit. Readings and meditations are good for the spirit. It is also important to learn what kinds of activities to avoid. "Temptation" is not a popular word anymore, even in books like this one. Thinking that we are tempted seems to imply a devil and some forces we cannot control. We like to think we are in control. But if we are honest most of us know we are subject to all sorts of forces that we find difficult to control. In today's world, our own greed and vanity are always near the surface. Each of us must look more closely to see what sinful tendencies are near.

The sin that Jesus objected to most strongly was that of the "righteous," those who considered themselves to be doing all the things that were prescribed by the Law. We have to be wary of temptations in this regard: thinking that we are better than others—because we go to church, our marriages are in good shape, we do not take drugs, and so on.

Jesus teaches us about God who wants us to approach in simplicity. We, like Matthew, are called. According to tradition, Matthew went from being a tax collector to being a writer of the gospel, writing of what Jesus said and did. The gospel bearing his name was undoubtedly put together using various sources and it reflects the faith of the earliest Jewish/Christian community. But it also bears the stamp of an individual mind and heart. Was it actually Levi/Matthew? We don't really know, but whoever it was, it was someone who was called and whose life was changed because he they listened and followed the call.

REFLECTION

Jesus has called you. The fact that you are reading books like this one is proof positive. This book is about responding to Jesus Christ, personally. What is Jesus asking of you? First to follow: to become better acquainted with Jesus who lived and still lives in God. You live in the life of God. Jesus also calls you to some particular tasks, and those tasks may be right in front of you or perhaps you will have to look a little further.

WEEKLY PRACTICE

Matthew brought the teachings of Jesus to others, particularly in recording the wonderful Sermon on the Mount. Reread these teachings of Jesus in chapters 5, 6, and 7 of Matthew's gospel and pray about how they invite you to live more fully in Jesus' life.

13

Marriage and Divorce

Jesus said to her, "Go, call your husband, and come back." The woman answered him, "I have no husband." Jesus said to her, "You are right in saying, 'I have no husband'; for you have had five husbands, and the one you have now is not your husband. What you have said is true!" [JOHN 4:16–18]

The brief encounters with Jesus on which we are reflecting are intended to increase your interest and curiosity so that you will go to your Bible and read the entire narrative. The verses above are taken from Jesus' meeting with a Samaritan woman. This is one of a number of extended encounters and conversations in John's gospel. Often they describe not only incidents from the life of Jesus but also issues in the early church. In this case, there were Samaritan Christians in the first-century church tracing their roots and establishing themselves as part of the new community of Jesus.

There are several curious themes in this encounter of the woman with Jesus. It begins with Jesus resting by himself, while his disciples go off for provisions, and a woman comes alone to draw water. Jesus asks her to give him a drink. The Jews and Samaritans had almost nothing to do with each other. And it would not be quite proper for a man alone to ask a woman alone for a drink. So, although the conversation started with these rather awkward circumstances, the topics then proceeded from water, to marriage, to salvation, to a community of faith.

Christian teaching and practice about marriage has a long and winding history. Jesus followed the Torah, going back to Genesis, teaching that man and woman were made for each other. He spoke strongly against divorce. Paul teaches that it is better to remain unmarried, but he further says that it is better to be married than to burn, presumably with desire. It is important to remember that Paul and the first generations of Christians were strongly influenced by their belief that they had entered the end-times, and whatever they did was conditioned by their expectation of the imminent return of Christ and the conclusion of this world as we know it.

The fathers of the Church generally taught that virginity and celibacy were preferable to marriage. In the early centuries there was no official Christian or church-related marriage ceremony. For many centuries in Europe, the ceremony was based on the laws and customs of the Roman Empire. During the tenth and eleventh centuries theologians and those engaged in ministry began to see the centrality of marriage and the family in living a Christian life. Matrimony became one of the sacraments. Settling on seven sacraments did not happen until the time of Thomas Aquinas in the thirteenth century.

Chaucer in the fourteenth century has the Wife of Bath saying, with regard to marriage, that people could learn about marriage through experience, even if there were no authority to teach us. She muses on the Samaritan woman and what happened to her husbands. She tells us that she herself has had five husbands, all of whom she married "at the church door," which was the custom at that time. Mass was then said within the church.

THE CHRISTIAN EXPERIENCE

We have some very strong statements from Jesus about divorce. But they must be understood in connection with the Torah, to which Jesus was committed. Gerhard Lohfink says that Jesus was not making a new rule or law but was speaking on behalf of women who were treated as property by the Law of Moses. Jesus was saying that it was not right for a man to dismiss his wife based simply on his own preferences, as was the custom at that time.

Where does this leave us as we seek an understanding of Christian life, marriage, and divorce? As we have said before, in working out how to live Christian lives, we have Scripture and the teachings of the church, and we also have our lived Christian experience. The Catholic Church has tried to hold fast to the rule that the bond of marriage is unbreakable and divorce is not permitted. The Protestant churches have recognized that marriages can break down and die, even becoming destructive for those involved. And the most recent Catholic teaching on the family states, "It is important that the divorced who have entered a new union should be made to feel part of the Church" (Pope Francis, *The Joy of Love*, 243). What this means is being worked out couple by couple and parish by parish.

But the challenges are many. It seems that contemporary living has placed very high expectations on married life and on the family. In this modern world we are urged to fulfill ourselves individually in every possible way, while also entering into relationships that will excite, satisfy, and complete us, and we are also expected to raise extraordinary children. Commercials and marketing practices tell us we should be enjoying heaven on earth, in our personal and family lives. No wonder people are sometimes disappointed in marriage.

REFLECTION

Marriages are more likely to succeed when they are embedded in a larger framework of church, community, friends, and love stretching in all directions. As church and as families, we are committed to a community of love, not laws. True love requires commitment and sacrifice.

WEEKLY PRACTICE

You undoubtedly have relatives and friends who are struggling with marriage and family issues. You don't need to be a therapist to help them in quiet ways. Jesus began his conversation with the Samaritan woman by asking for a drink of water. Then they talked about marriage and faith and worship. Marriage, for Jesus, was embedded in the wider world of relationships and faith. And so it should be for us. It is almost certain that this week you will have opportunities to help people with their marriages.

= 14 =

The Life
to Come

*The same day some Sadducees came to him, saying,...
"Now there were seven brothers among us; the first
married, and died childless, leaving the widow to his
brother. The second did the same, so also the third,
down to the seventh. Last of all, the woman herself died.
In the resurrection, then, whose wife of the seven will
she be? For all of them had married her."*

*Jesus answered them, "You are wrong, because you
know neither the scriptures nor the power of God. For
in the resurrection they neither marry nor are given in
marriage, but are like angels in heaven. And as for the
resurrection of the dead, have you not read what was
said to you by God, 'I am the God of Abraham, the God
of Isaac, and the God of Jacob'? He is the God not of the
dead, but of the living."* [MATTHEW 22:23-32]

Questions about life after death have been asked and
in some ways answered by peoples throughout history. It is difficult to know just what the ancient
Egyptians believed. But they went to extraordinary lengths

to embalm the pharaohs, preserving their bodies and inner organs. And of course they built enormous tombs to house their remains in preparation for some future life. It seems that respect for the dead and belief in some form of afterlife may be universal among humans.

Where were the Sadducees coming from when they posed the question to Jesus? We are told that they were a very strict, observant group among the priestly class. They did not, however, believe in the resurrection—not because they were liberal thinkers, but because they did not find clear teaching of a resurrected afterlife in the Torah, the teachings of Moses that guided their thinking. So it seems they were testing Jesus, proposing a case with a dilemma—assuming that the afterlife is like this one.

Jesus takes their concern seriously and answers them in the Rabbinic tradition, using both reason and the Scriptures. He tells them that the resurrected body will be different from our earthly bodies. We see this in Jesus' own resurrection; and the idea occurs a number of times in the teachings of Paul. The risen body, Paul teaches, will be imperishable, and so it is essentially different from the body we have now. He says that the difference between our earthly bodies and the resurrected body is like the difference between a seed and the flower or plant that grows from it. This is indeed a big difference.

But then Jesus talks about the power of God, quoting God's words when Moses wants to know who God is. In one of the most dramatic moments in the Old Testament, God in the apparition of the burning bush tells Moses that he is the God of Abraham, Isaac, and Jacob. Jesus ends by saying that God is the God of the living. Is Jesus saying that Abraham, Isaac, and Jacob are still living—and so God is the God of the living?

Or perhaps he is saying that we have enough to worry about in considering our connection to God in this life. We have the promise of the resurrection; what that exactly means is beyond our comprehension—but not beyond our faith.

There are, however, a number of ways in which we can think about our lives beyond the material world and our bodies. To the philosophers of ancient Greece, it was evident that the soul is a non-material part of our being. They believed that since we can think in terms of concepts that are universal—and these concepts transcend the material world—we therefore must have a non-material soul or spirit within us. To them, values such as love and justice were further evidence of the soul.

Christian philosophers and theologians adopted the idea of the spiritual soul. It helped explain what we find in Scripture. The general teaching has been that, when we die, the body disintegrates, returning to the earth from which it came, but the soul lives on—to be united with the resurrected body at the end of time.

Whatever the risen body might be like, the Christian tradition is very strong in emphasizing that we live in community with those who have gone before us. With this in mind the Catholic tradition identified saints as guides, protectors, and models for varied occupations and circumstances.

THE CHRISTIAN EXPERIENCE

Consider Rose Hawthorne, a woman who is at the core of American and Christian life. She was born in 1851, the third daughter of Nathaniel Hawthorne. She married and had a son, who died at the age of four. She later separated from her alcoholic husband. She entered into nursing, and after her husband died she founded the Dominican Sisters of Hawthorne, Congregation of Saint Rose of Lima, providing nursing care to those afflicted with incurable cancer who are unable to afford nursing care elsewhere.

In the materials prepared for her beatification, Gabriel O'Donnell, OP, wrote, "Service to Christ's poor did not simply mean that this lady of culture, education and social status would put on an apron and offer gifts from her abundance. She decided to live among the poor, to beg for them as they did for themselves, and to establish a home where they could live in dignity, cleanliness, and ease as they faced their final days on earth." Rose Hawthorne was an inspiration for Dorothy Day and for Hospice, accomplishing as much after her death as in her life.

REFLECTION AND WEEKLY PRACTICE

The words of Jesus, "He is the God not of the dead but of the living," are rich with meaning. What might the statement mean for you? One meaning might be: *this is where you are; attend to your life as you live it now.* The best thing you and I can do is to care for one another—the sick, the needy, the refugee, the addict, all those who need help and love. There are many such people near and far. It is for you and me to show them that God cares and is with them. What will happen to us after death is in God's hands; our work is here and now—to be accepted and accomplished for God, who is the God of the living.

= **15** =

The One Who Is to Come

When John heard in prison what the Messiah was doing, he sent word by his disciples and said to him, "Are you the one who is to come, or are we to wait for another?" Jesus answered them, "Go and tell John what you hear and see: the blind receive their sight, the lame walk, the lepers are cleansed, the deaf hear, the dead are raised, and the poor have good news brought to them. And blessed is anyone who takes no offense at me."

[MATTHEW 11:2–6]

We have noted the close relationship between John and Jesus. John announced Jesus and perhaps was his mentor. They preached similar messages of renewal. They believed that the days were at hand for the fulfillment of God's promises to Israel. So what happened to John that he could ask, "or are we to wait for another?"

Perhaps we should look first at Jesus' last sentence: "And blessed is anyone who takes no offense at me." Were John's expectations not met? Was he hoping for something more or different from Jesus? He was languishing in prison while Jesus preached, healed, and brought hope. Like many at the time, perhaps John expected a political change, or maybe he anticipated a role for himself in this new dispensation. Or he may have wondered why Jesus with his compassion and his power could not do something for him.

With the harshness of his situation in prison, it would be human for him to doubt, to wonder if he was mistaken in giving his heart and soul to Jesus. Did he perhaps doubt his own mission and the whole direction of his life? Like Jesus a few years later in the garden, was he asking that this misery be taken from him? We don't know the answers to these questions, but we have to believe that his faith and Jesus' response strengthened him.

THE CHRISTIAN EXPERIENCE

What about us? As committed Christians we have given our minds and hearts to God in Jesus Christ. But we have many needs and wants and responsibilities that seem to take us in other directions. Some things are sinful, and we try to steer away from them. Perhaps even when we pray, when we recommit ourselves to Christ, do we sometimes wonder, "Are you the one?" And then we wonder about the meaning of our own lives.

Over the centuries, Christians have asked how Jesus fits in to this very secular and science-based world of ours. Alfred North Whitehead, in his book *Science in the Modern World*, proposes that natural science arose in the West, largely in Europe, because of two fundamental ideas related to Judaism and Christianity: first, the conviction that all of creation comes from a good and rational God who shares with us. And second, this sharing reached its peak when God, in Christ, entered into our world, becoming one of us, taking on matter. So matter cannot be evil or foreign to our destiny—as was sometimes believed in the ancient world. The world around us is both orderly and worth studying, even spending a lifetime asking and answering questions.

Scientists and science have answered many questions, explaining a great deal of the world around us and giving a better understanding of our own lives. Some have said that we don't need a god to explain the origins of diseases and how to cure people. We don't need a god to explain the weather, storms, and the destruction that comes. We don't need a god to explain the multiplicity of animals in our world. We have science. We as humans have found that we do not need God to explain many aspects of the world around us or to answer many of the questions we pose about our lives. Some people were led to describe a God who created the universe, giving it a start, but then stepped back, letting the laws and processes of nature take over.

And yet as individuals and as a human race, we are troubled. Science has not brought us peace or harmony or quietness of spirit. Shall we continue to "look for another"? We suffer from a nagging fear that we are not worth very much, that we are wandering in a desert without direction. We think that if we only had more money or things, if we had only accomplished something wonderful. So as individuals and as a people we wonder where to look. Science has indeed provided easier lives, but it has also promoted death and destruction. Even those who are most fortunate with material privileges often seem pessimistic, without hope or confidence.

What of the arts? Through the ages people have expressed themselves, providing insights into life and offering us beauty through art, music, and literature. Shakespeare explored and described human relationships and human emotions. We read or watch *King Lear* and we say, "Yes, how many families have been torn apart over inheritance?" It does not have to be that way. We read or watch *Hamlet* and reflect on our own uncertainty in the face of evil. We contemplate a Vermeer painting and catch our breath as we contemplate the wonders in each moment of life. And yet, even these thoughts and emotions are not fully satisfying; they lead us to think that there is more, somehow. Poetry and novels and all of the arts. They lead us to grasp something of the beauty in this life and the conviction that we are made to participate in something more.

And how did Jesus answer John's question? What did he tell those who came asking, "Are you the one? Or should we look for another?"

Jesus lists spectacular and miraculous happenings, building up to the raising of the dead, and this in the gospels always refers also to his own resurrection. And he concludes saying, "the poor have the good news preached to them." It seems that the poor accepting the gospel message is not simply a sign of Christ's compassion; it is the goal and purpose of his mission—his crowning achievement. Along with his resurrection, that "the poor have the good news preached to them" is a sign that the kingdom of God is among us.

REFLECTION AND WEEKLY PRACTICE

Science and art and friends and family and work—these are important parts of life. But in in Jesus' mind, his greatest work was that "the poor have the good news preached to them." This was and remains the sign that God is active in our midst. What does this mean to you and to me? The poor? In what ways do we show our concern for the poor? How have I tried to preach the good news to the poor? What is the good news and how do you and I preach it in today's world? These are difficult questions. I cannot answer them for you. We must pray individually and together that Christ our Lord will help us find a way to "preach" the good news to the poor.

16

The Time

So when they had come together, they asked him, "Lord, is this the time when you will restore the kingdom to Israel?" He replied, "It is not for you to know the times or periods that the Father has set by his own authority. But you will receive power when the Holy Spirit has come upon you; and you will be my witnesses in Jerusalem, in all Judea and Samaria, and to the ends of the earth." [ACTS 1:6–8]

This exchange is the last recorded conversation between Jesus and his closest disciples. We know that the kingdom, with all its mystery, was central in Jesus' message and in his efforts to bring his followers to God, in community. And yet here, even after his resurrection, they yearn for a restoration of the nation with the glories of Israel past.

Jesus in response takes the conversation in a different direction, as he so often did. The Father has plans, and we are included, but they are beyond our understanding. Not only that, but in the next sentence Jesus implicitly tells his followers that it is not knowledge of future events that matters but what they themselves are to do. And he tells them what that will be. They will receive power from the Holy Spirit and will be witnesses "to the ends of the earth." Luke Timothy Johnson, discussing activities described in the Acts of the Apostles, says that the human church was frequently catching up with the actions of the Holy Spirit.

The Holy Spirit did indeed come over Jesus' followers. In fact, the Acts of the Apostles might be called the Acts of the Holy Spirit. Witnessing and the Holy Spirit are closely linked. When the high priest and council of elders called in Peter, saying they had ordered him not to teach, Peter spoke about the death and resurrection of Jesus, the forgiveness of sins. He concluded, "And we are witnesses to these things, and so is the Holy Spirit whom God has given to those who obey him" (Acts 5:32). Peter puts himself in the company of the Holy Spirit as a witness. We, like Peter, are called to work with the Holy Spirit.

THE CHRISTIAN EXPERIENCE

One of the first Christian documents, beyond the New Testament writings, is called the *Didache*, probably written toward the end of the first century. It is a mini-catechism, providing instruction about how to live and the administration of the sacraments and describing some of the early practices of Christian communities. The writing reflects the gospels and provides a rich source for prayer and reflection. It begins as follows.

1. There are two Ways, one of Life and one of Death, and there is a great difference between the two Ways.

2. The way of life is this: "First, you shall love the God

who made thee, secondly, thy neighbor as thyself; and whatsoever thou wouldst not have done to thyself, do not thou to another."

3. Now, the teaching of these words is this: "Bless those that curse you, and pray for your enemies, and fast for those that persecute you. For what credit is it to you if you love those that love you? Do not even the heathen do the same?" But, for your part, "love those that hate you," and you will have no enemy.

The document takes the words of Jesus and expands them, giving fresh insights. The *Didache*, like the Acts of the Apostles, speaks of the Way: Christians are called followers of the Way. This is a beautiful symbol, implying a journey, leadership, and community.

The second paragraph includes what we have come to call the Golden Rule, but by pointing to what we should avoid, what we should not do. The two forms are equivalent, but in practice there can be differences. Particularly in our modern world, with all its greed and deceit, it is important to be on guard and to remember that what we do has consequences. We do not like other people to gossip about us in mean ways; we would not want others to cheat in their work for us; we would not want people to tell us half-truths or lies in order to gain our approval. So we should avoid these and many other ways of acting that we would not like done to us and that weaken the fabric of community.

Paragraph 3 directs us to "fast for those that persecute you." Fasting is recommended or recounted many times in both the Old and New Testaments—as an act of repentance (e.g., David after his sin), in seeking God's blessing, in time of famine or disease, and in general to show one's faithfulness, acknowledging that we belong to God. In more modern terms it has been said that to overcome our unruly human nature, we must do something more. Fasting takes us beyond the daily routine of moderation in eating. In the situation recounted above, fasting is considered a kind of prayer that might be offered to God on behalf of another.

We still today discuss Jesus' instruction that his followers become witnesses. For centuries Christians have believed that care, frugality, even fasting—eating less than one needs—these things show others that we believe there is much more to life than what we eat and what we wear. We are, at the roots of our lives, spiritual beings.

REFLECTION

There are many ways to be witnesses to Jesus Christ. Just as Jesus' own interactions with those around him varied from day to day, so also our witnessing will vary. We may witness by offering words of consolation or advice. We may help someone in need. Whatever we do should be done by keeping in contact with the Holy Spirit, remembering that we together with the Holy Spirit are witnesses to the great works of Jesus and to the kingdom that is among us.

WEEKLY PRACTICE

You will have opportunities this week to be a witness to Jesus Christ. Don't let them pass. It may be in political discussion, in family conversations, at work, or in entertainment. Things are not as they were in the Acts of the Apostles. We live in a world that in many ways has grown tired of the Christian message. How can we make it fresh and meaningful? Think just for five to ten minutes each morning about how you can be a witness to Jesus Christ that day.

═ 17 ═

Jesus Looked at Him

He said to him, "Teacher, I have kept all these since my youth." Jesus, looking at him, loved him and said, "You lack one thing; go, sell what you own, and give the money to the poor, and you will have treasure in heaven; then come, follow me." When he heard this, he was shocked and went away grieving, for he had many possessions. [MARK 10:20-22]

Jesus did not ask or require the same from everyone he met. He listened and sized up the person and the situation. After miracles or brief interactions, some persons followed him, some went back to their towns, some stayed home until he visited again, and perhaps some forgot about him. So it has been through the ages. Jesus with the power of the Spirit invites us; we respond—in different ways.

You will recall that the verses above occur in several of the gospels. Often called the "Rich Young Man," the episode begins with a man asking Jesus what he must do. Jesus tells him that the commandments are clear. The man says he wants to do more. Jesus tells him and it is too much for the man; he goes away sad.

For those who wish to follow, to imitate, "to be perfect,"

there are no half measures. Jesus spoke in terms so absolute, so demanding, that they cannot be codified into rules and laws. "Do not worry about tomorrow." "Sell what you own and give the money to the poor." "If anyone strikes you on the right cheek, turn the other cheek also."

THE CHRISTIAN EXPERIENCE

Leo Tolstoy, meditating on Jesus' way of speaking, believed that the teaching church had betrayed the message, finding it easier in many ways to create rules that seem to comply with the radical message than to accept and live the message in a more radical form. To Tolstoy, this thinking undermined what Jesus invites us to do and to become. His essay, "The Kingdom of God Is within You," has been influential in awakening people to the gospel.

> "One ought not to expect so much," is what people usually say in discussing the requirements of the Christian religion. "One cannot expect to take absolutely no thought for the morrow, as is said in the gospel, but only not to take so much thought for it; one cannot give away all to the poor, but one must give away a certain definite part; one need not aim at virginity, but one must avoid debauchery; one need not forsake wife and children, but one must not give too great a place to them in one's heart," and so on.
>
> But to speak like this is just like telling a man who is struggling on a swift river and is directing his course against the current, that it is impossible to cross the river rowing against the current, and that to cross it he must float in the direction of the point he wants to reach.

In reality, in order to reach the place to which he wants to go, he must row with all his strength toward a point much higher up.

Through the ages, the Church has often analyzed the commandments and teachings of Jesus in a legalistic way, devising rules to follow Jesus but consistent with the demands of life as it is lived.

"Thou shall not kill." But it is important to defend yourself, even to the point of killing the one who is attacking you. It may be necessary to execute someone to preserve the common good. War is bad but permissible under certain conditions. And so it is with the other commandments. We consider conditions and circumstances.

But Jesus was not a lawyer. His teachings are unconditional. This does not mean, however, that they are always to be taken literally.

"If your eye offend you, pluck it out." We all know that Jesus did not intend this to be taken literally. But he intended it to be taken seriously. We should be very careful about what we see, what we read. How many advertisements do we see every day? And what are they doing to us? That is for each of us to judge.

Some of Jesus' uncompromising, unconditional statements should be taken very seriously. "Do not worry, saying, 'What will we eat?' or 'What will we drink? or 'What will we wear?'" How much time and energy do we spend worrying about exactly these things? Vanity and greed are lurking everywhere, all the time. What are we to do? Jesus gives us the answer: "Strive first for the kingdom of God and his righteousness, and all these things will be given to you as well" (Matthew 6:33).

REFLECTION

Like the young man in the story we are considering, we ask Jesus every day what we are to do. And every day we walk away sad because we have possessions. But on the following day Jesus is there once again, waiting, perhaps even smiling, as we ask once again, "What must I do to inherit eternal life?"

And Jesus looks at us with love.

"Stop worrying," he tells us. "It will not do you any good. Give to those in need. Money will not save you. When you die, I, Jesus, the Lord, will not look at your bank account. I will look into your heart."

Jesus asked different things of different people. And so it has been through history. Each of us must examine our possessions, considering whether they are bringing us closer to the Lord or creating barriers.

WEEKLY PRACTICE

Examine your conscience considering the things you own. Are they too much? Should you share them with those in need? Consider the way you use your time? Can you pray and meditate more? Can you help those in need? Consider your words and how you can use them to build up the kingdom of God.

PART III

JESUS IS IN CHARGE

Real leaders do not have to prove themselves over and over. They can be friendly, down to earth, and good listeners. So it was with Jesus. But there are moments when a leader must show who he is and what he is made of. Jesus ordered an evil spirit to leave a man. And those around him marveled, "Who is this that the evil spirits obey him?" In another incident, the Pharisees criticize Jesus for not observing the pre-meal washings. Jesus did not get into a debate with them; he said simply that they neglect the commandments of God while keeping their traditions.

What about us? Are there indeed evil spirits among us? Do we have the courage to cast them out? Christ our Lord gives us the strength to do that—if we will only believe and pray. The traditions! How sidetracked do we get with our traditions? In the following readings and reflections, we see Jesus Christ, human and divine, in moments of strength and decisiveness.

= **18** =

Becoming
the Other

"If you choose, you can make me clean." Moved with
pity, Jesus stretched out his hand and touched him
and said to him, "I do choose. Be made clean!"

[**MARK 1:40-41**]

Jesus takes the words of the leper and repeats them.
The repetition or echo of something said by another
can be satisfying, particularly in the spoken word. This is
true of the psalms. Verses very often repeat a thought.

Give ear to my words, O Lord;
give heed to my sighing.
Listen to the sound of my cry,
my King and my God,
for to you I pray. [**PSALM 5:1-2**]

Repeating the petition with different words focuses the mind:
"Give ear to my words; listen to the sound of my cry." How
can God not listen, hear, and attend to us. But the psalms
are not always easy for us. They come from a distant cul-

ture. Saying them aloud, however, even when alone is always rewarding.

The repetitive character makes the psalms suitable for alternative, antiphonal speaking or singing, as is often done in churches and monasteries.

Repetition reinforces mutual love and commitment. In a somewhat similar way, the president repeating the words of the oath of office, phrase by phrase, adds solemnity to the occasion and to the oath. Reading it or even having it memorized would not have the same impact.

Something similar happens in a wedding ceremony. It is pleasing for bride and groom and for those attending to hear the same words repeated.

> I, (*name*), take you, (*name*), to be my (*husband/wife*). I promise to be faithful to you, in good times and in bad, in sickness and in health, to love you and to honor you all the days of my life.

Through words and sometimes through actions we can become the other person. The renewal of vows is another way in which both partners repeat their promises and commitment.

In Mark Twain's book *The Prince and the Pauper*, the young prince of England invites a poor beggar boy into his rooms at the palace. For fun the two change clothes and then notice that they are very alike in appearance. A servant comes and, despite their protestations, throws the prince, dressed like a beggar, out of the palace. The rest of the book explores the adventures and experiences of the two as they learn about each other's lives, families, and habits.

In echoing the phrase of the man with leprosy, Jesus was saying that he not only understood but also wanted to put himself in the sick man's place: *"You say that if I choose, yes I do choose. I will take your words and with them enter into your life, healing you."*

Even in everyday conversation, repeating a phrase adds a sense of intimacy, "Would you like to get together for lunch?" "I *would* like to get together for lunch." A small thing, perhaps, but in a way we are not only accepting the invitation; in using the same words we become the other person.

In the incident we are discussing, Jesus does more than repeat the man's words; he touches the man. Jesus was not afraid of leprosy. It might have been just as important to the man that Jesus touched him as it was that he was cured of his skin disease. People did not touch lepers. Even now we might feel repugnance at rashes and diseases of the skin. We are not likely to touch them. But Jesus touched the man.

And the man went out proclaiming what Jesus had done for him. Like many of the people in the gospel stories, we don't hear any more of him. But we might imagine that he became one of the earliest Christians, telling others how, when Jesus used his very words to cure him, he felt connected, attached, to this man, his Lord, sent from God.

We can be sure that this man whom Jesus touched and cured understood when Paul preached,

> I have been crucified with Christ; and it is no longer I who live, but it is Christ who lives in me. And the life I now live in the flesh I live by faith in the Son of God, who loved me and gave himself for me. [GALATIANS 2:19-20]

We can imagine how the former leper would have appreciated these words. He would say to himself, "My flesh was made clean by the Christ. He touched me. Now I have become part of him."

This is the great mystery of Christianity, also explored by Paul using the image of the body. Christ belongs to God, and we belong to Christ. We share his life. We are connected to Christ and to one another. That does not make us all the same. We have many roles to play and responsibilities to accept. Individually and together, we are part of Christ.

We are justified and yet we remain sinners. Like the leper, we must come to Christ with total confidence, telling him, "If you choose, you can make me clean." And over and over he will clean us of our selfishness, of our greed, and of the ill- nesses that only he knows.

The story ends with Jesus telling the man not to tell any- one. The man goes away, and the gospel says that he told so many people that great crowds came wherever Jesus went so that he couldn't even enter the towns. Those studying the gospels have wondered why Jesus on a number of occasions told people not to spread the word about miracles or about who he was. They have posed the question and theory of "the messianic secret." Perhaps Jesus did not want his identity known before it was time, lest he be killed before he was able to explain his mission and the kingdom and how the Messiah differed from people's expectations.

Perhaps Jesus, who was fully human, needed time to pray, to teach, to choose his followers. He did not want to be over- whelmed by crowds. But the man immediately did the oppo- site of what Jesus instructed. We should remember that Jesus also told him to show himself to the priests so that he might be declared clean, according to the Law of Moses. So the man received somewhat mixed signals and followed his heart.

REFLECTION

We also should make known what Jesus has done for us. Jesus has entered our lives and through us will come to others. Even if we say nothing, people will think, "So you are a Christian," and they will wonder what it means. And we shall enter into their lives. One of the obstacles to "becoming the other" is tribalism. In our day, this ancient feeling seems to be emerging with new intensity. Tribalism, that very strong feeling of identity with "my group" combined with hostility toward others for whom we feel resentment, may be based on political, ethnic, or religious identity.

WEEKLY PRACTICE

We have to search our souls and pray diligently to escape tribalism. It is contrary to everything Jesus lived for and everything he continues to teach us. This week, ask yourself in prayer and meditation how you favor those in your "group," whatever that might mean. Look for ways to appreciate those who seem to be different. You will be rewarded. Christ our Lord is in everyone, wanting to show us God's love.

⟹ 19 ⟸

Compassion

Then Peter came and said to him, "Lord, if another
member of the church sins against me, how often should
I forgive? As many as seven times?" Jesus said to him,
"Not seven times, but, I tell you, seventy-seven times."
[MATTHEW 18:21–22]

ased on the ancient texts, there is debate about
whether Jesus' response included "seventy times
seven," as many of us remember from first hearing
the passage, or "seventy-seven," not as a large number, but
still a lot when it comes to forgiving.

We notice that Jesus is called by different names and titles.
"Teacher" is common. In this case, Peter, recognizing Jesus'
very special connection to God, calls him "Lord," which for
the Jews of the time was sometimes used for the name of
God. Peter, in asking his question, acknowledges that forgiveness comes from or is rooted in God.

Jesus' response is a number too large to keep track of.
He is saying that there is no limit, that we should not try to
count such things. We all know how we bristle when someone brings up a number: "Now that is the third time this week
you have..." As Jesus suggests in the Lord's Prayer, we should

seek to participate in the boundless goodness and forgiveness of God.

We have to believe that Jesus found the answer to many questions in his prolonged prayer. As fully human he strengthened his connection to God, and that is what we must do too. Forgiveness is only the first step. Prayer and love turn forgiveness to compassion.

Love of God is expressed in prayer, which is real contact with God. God wants us to make this contact and to maintain it—not for just an odd moment but for some extended time each day. Unfortunately, most of us cannot find this time. (One spiritual director said that we should meditate for twenty minutes a day, except on days when we do not have the time; then we should meditate for an hour.) If we do pray more earnestly and more frequently, we will find the love of God flowing more fully into our lives. We will begin to make decisions and plans with God's interests and concerns in our minds and hearts.

Men and women who love their spouses and partners, who care deeply for each other—such people do not have to spend time thinking about whether being unfaithful will hurt a spouse or whether wasting money will injure the family, or whether a mean word will damage a relationship. They avoid these things without thinking or calculating. If we are in touch with God, and if we nourish that contact through prayer, we will live so that that love becomes stronger. Jesus commented that one who looked on a woman with lust had committed adultery in his heart. Love and forgiveness are expressed in action, but they originate in the heart.

We show our love for God by loving our neighbor. We cannot love God and break trust with our neighbor by lying. We cannot love God and injure our neighbor, who carries the image of God. We cannot love God and use sexual activities simply to make us feel good, toying with the affections and trust of others.

And so, the contract proposed by Jesus in the Our Father and repeated each time we say the prayer—that God's forgiveness toward us is conditioned by our forgiveness of others—is not an arbitrary rule set down by God. It is rather in the nature of things. In wronging others, we wrong the creator who made them and who lives in them. Similarly, if we have been wronged, we have the opportunity to share in the merciful forgiving power of God by forgiving others the wrongs they have done to us.

We have all seen or read about the spouse or parent of a victim who visits jail to express forgiveness to the killer of a loved one. We have undoubtedly also asked ourselves if we could possibly express such forgiveness. Fortunately, most of us are not called upon to act in such circumstances. But we have many opportunities to forgive in smaller ways.

First, we have to forgive those close to us, and mean it. Children, as they grow, and even when grown, can harbor grudges against their parents for all sorts of real and imagined wrongs. Similarly, parents can become cold and distant to children who do not live as their parents had hoped.

Between relatives, friends, coworkers, and neighborhood acquaintances, minor differences can harden into permanent ways of acting and thinking. A thaw becomes difficult. Brothers and sisters, neighbors, those on the job together can go years without speaking, visiting, or forgiving. The Our Father reminds us, as Jesus did, to seek out those we have injured or who have injured us and find reconciliation.

Gandhi, as portrayed in the film, encountered a Hindu man, greatly distressed and grieving because he has killed a

Muslim man, leaving his young son an orphan. "What should I do?" he asks the great religious leader. Gandhi tells him to take the child, care for him, and raise him—as a Muslim. To really forgive and to seek forgiveness we must enter into the lives of others.

Recent years have seen a rise in efforts to accept and appreciate "diversity," that is, people whose ethnicity or lifestyle is different from our own. But appreciating differences is not enough; we must strive to recognize and build on the deeply rooted common bonds that we share as humans, children of the one God. We have heard the gospel stories so often that we might fail to appreciate that Jesus had a vision of love and compassion across differences: Jews and Samaritans did not socialize at all; tax collectors were viewed as collaborators, not to be trusted; many of the poor were not observant of the regular, expected religious practices. But Jesus made a Samaritan the exemplar of concern; he selected a tax collector to be one of his intimate followers; he announced that the kingdom he was ushering in would belong to the poor.

REFLECTION

We should ask God to turn the light of justice on our world, to help us recognize injustice—in others and in ourselves. We are guilty of wrongs. We have done evil and are sorry. We have neglected to do good, and we want to change. We need not be depressed or filled with self-pity. God in Christ Jesus has forgiven us. He puts our wrongs behind us. He will not look upon them anymore.

WEEKLY PRACTICE

Jesus has been called "the Compassion of God." And compassion is what Jesus tells us to show one another. Compassion means "to suffer with" or to "bear with." We should not count wrongs. We need to act with the generosity and large-heartedness that God shows us and that comes from God. This week consider those from whom you should seek forgiveness. Find at least one person and tell them you are sorry.

20

A Better View

So he ran ahead and climbed a sycamore tree to see him, because he was going to pass that way. When Jesus came to the place, he looked up and said to him, "Zacchaeus, hurry and come down; for I must stay at your house today." [LUKE 19:4-5]

The story also tells us that Zacchaeus was short and there was a large crowd around Jesus. Still, it is unusual for a grown man to climb a tree, and it was probably unusual in Jesus' time too. What kind of man climbs a tree in this situation? It seems likely that Zacchaeus was impetuous and not concerned about what other people thought. The story also says he was rich. I think we can picture this kind of man—a bit loud, self-made we might say, curious about the one who attracted crowds: Jesus, who spoke in wondrous paradoxes and healed the sick.

With regard to Jesus, we don't have to imagine that he used divine knowledge to know Zacchaeus's name or what he was about. Everyone around him was talking. "Oh, there goes Zacchaeus. What is he up to this time? Up in a tree; you might know. Tax collector he is; he's left a few people up a tree himself."

Jesus looks up and calls to him. He, Jesus, wants to go with Zacchaeus to his house, to join him and his friends at a meal. Zacchaeus is excited, honored, and pleased. But some grumble. He is a sinner; he doesn't observe the traditions.

Zacchaeus knows what Jesus preaches: giving to the poor, being just. Zacchaeus says he will give half his belongings to the poor and will repay, four times over, anyone he has cheated. Jesus is pleased that salvation has come to this house; he has come for the lost, for sinners.

We might go back for a minute and reflect on what Zacchaeus did and how it might relate to us. He climbed a tree to gain a better view of Jesus.

What are the things that get in the way and obstruct our view of Jesus? There is talk these days about simplifying. All of us recognize that "stuff'" gets in the way of our view, our peace of mind, our sense of direction in life. In a Christian sense, the saints and mystics have always talked about simplifying, about clearing away the things that obstruct our view and our ability to follow Jesus.

It starts with possessions, things, using, owning. How much time and effort and attention do we give to clothes and jewelry and money and efforts to gain the approval of those around us, even to satisfy our own sense of worth? These things can get in the way of having a good view of the Jesus of the gospels.

And then there are amusements of every kind. How many hours do we idle away with TV and computers? These things may not be evil, but they get in the way of the vision we should be seeking.

Zacchaeus, like the Apostle Matthew, was a tax collector, not respected by those around him; to them he was a sinner. But Jesus did not see it that way. He welcomed and still welcomes those of different professions, even those doing less respected kinds of work. Zacchaeus was overwhelmed that this prophet would visit his home. Jesus did not generally talk in half measures. "Go sell what you have and give the money to the poor," he said to the rich young man.

But in this case he does not fault Zacchaeus. Jesus knows that the man is doing what he can. Perhaps he knows that Zacchaeus will use the remaining money to do good. And Zacchaeus as much as admits that he has defrauded people, promising to make it up fourfold.

THE CHRISTIAN EXPERIENCE

The message for us, of course, is to open our minds and hearts and bank accounts to the poor. We might admire the billionaires who have given or promised to give half of all they own to charitable causes. But in the back of our mind we also think, well, they have billions; I only have...so much.

It reminds me of Samuel Johnson who commented on the Levellers, a group of socialist-type thinkers. Johnson said that, in his experience, Levellers wanted to level things down to themselves but could not bear to level up to themselves. Aren't we all subject to that kind of thinking? Yes, if I had a lot more money, then I would give generously. Those with a lot more than I have should give more. What I earn is not excessive; no one should earn much more than I do.

And what of Jesus' response to Zacchaeus? It seems, reading the gospels, that Jesus was always available. By contrast, when we call or are called for an appointment or a dinner engagement, we have to check our calendars and see when we are free—we have a lot going on.

We live in a different world, but still we should try every day to adopt that availability that was deep in Jesus' soul. In the parable of the Good Samaritan, Jesus tells us that the one who showed compassion, the Samaritan, was on a journey. But he interrupted it because of something more important. In another brief bit of advice, Jesus tells his followers that if they are about to offer sacrifice and remember any offense, they should leave the sacrifice and go ask for forgiveness. This sense of urgency and availability was a central quality of the apostle Paul. His belief in the imminent return of Jesus may have been mistaken if taken as a historical conviction, but Paul was urged on by something else: the kingdom of God is among us and calls on us to respond—now.

REFLECTION AND WEEKLY PRACTICE

Like Zacchaeus, we should climb the tree of faith today. When we do we will gain a better and clearer view of Jesus and what he expects of us. What are the obstacles in the way of your view of Jesus, his message, and his example? In what ways do you worry about embarrassing yourself or looking foolish? Zacchaeus didn't worry about those things. He didn't mind that people thought he was a bit ridiculous. He wanted to see Jesus.

≡ 21 ≡

The Stones Would
Shout Out

Some of the Pharisees in the crowd said to him, "Teacher, order your disciples to stop." He answered, "I tell you, if these were silent, the stones would shout out."

[LUKE 19:39–40]

This exchange takes place at the time of Jesus' triumphal entry into Jerusalem. The procession and celebration are still mysterious. Why did Jesus arrange this event? We mark it as Palm Sunday, the beginning of the week of Jesus' suffering, death, and resurrection. Palm Sunday seems natural to us as a sign of Jesus' final victory. And perhaps that is how he intended it, knowing that this earthly, ephemeral celebration would be transformed in a most mysterious way—by a seemingly tragic death that led to victory and to God's ultimate approval.

But why did these Pharisees tell Jesus to hush his disciples? Luke does not say. Perhaps the Pharisees as guardians of orthodoxy did not favor this new, freedom-loving preacher. His teaching might undermine the centrality of the temple and the Torah. Or perhaps they were jealous of his popularity. Whatever their motives and desires, they did not have the strength to confront the crowds themselves; they went to Jesus.

And what does his response—that the stones would shout out—mean? At first, we might think that the statement is a simple exaggeration—like saying that nature itself approves of what Jesus is doing. But we must remember that as this verbal exchange takes place, Jesus is moving toward the temple in his physical and spiritual journey, and the temple was central to Jewish faith.

We should also keep in mind that by the time the gospel was written the temple had been destroyed. And so, as writers often do, the evangelists include knowledge of what has happened in the interim when they write about past events. The destruction of the temple was a monumental event for Jews. It marked the end of their homeland. And it was highly significant for the early church. It was one more indication that Christianity, while rooted in Judea and Galilee, was destined to travel the world.

What do we think of ancient monuments like the Jerusalem temple? The Roman ruins amaze us. They speak to us of engineers, travelers, empires, and a way of life that is distant and yet familiar. Percy Bysshe Shelly's sonnet "Ozymandias" tells of the remains of a colossal statue, the legs still standing but the trunk and head resting in the sand. All around is a wasteland. And on the pedestal is written, "My name is Ozymandias, King of Kings: Look on my Works ye Mighty and despair!" The words as part of the poem are meant in irony. Once the despair would have been caused by the power of this king; but then the despair comes from his fall.

So it is. Nations and empires rise and fall. And the stones do indeed speak to us. They tell us that we are part of a great human enterprise. We encounter Greek-style columns every day—in public buildings, churches, and homes. They represent a remarkable combination of strength, beauty, and history. These stones speak to us of the origins of western philosophy, democracy, art, and public life. If we fail to listen to the stones we risk a great loss. Christianity has tried to incorporate what is best in different cultures and at times found itself in conflict with science, art, or politics.

Stones also speak to us in medieval cathedrals. They are magnificent testimonies to faith, art, and Christian tradition. Their spires lift our minds and hearts; their stained-glass windows instruct and inspire. And yet now they are often museums and monuments rather than places of worship. In spite of them, religious wars raged, inquisitions took place, and Europeans abandoned many Christian traditions. Just a few days ago, from this writing, the cathedral of Notre Dame in Paris suffered a great fire. Those of every nation and ethnicity expressed their sorrow, and this is testimony to the common bonds we feel in the great works of those who have gone before us.

And yet, perhaps the cathedrals are also telling us something not so different from Ozymandias. We should be wary about putting our trust in monuments, in stones, in church buildings. Some of our Christian traditions have indeed become very attached to our local churches or to our meeting houses. Those who "go to church" are judged to be faithful Christians.

But God is not to be contained within structures made by human hands. The God to whom we pray is more real and greater than the universe and is also within our hearts. We should indeed gather together in our churches to pray and to help one another along the journey of faith. But our lives of faith are lived mostly outside the building—with our families, in the marketplace, in the arena of work and politics, and among those in need.

THE CHRISTIAN EXPERIENCE

Finally, we might consider the stones and wood of our own homes. Though modest, most of us take pride in our surroundings, our furniture, our kitchens, and "all the comforts of home." This may not be wrong. But if we listen closely we will hear the stones and boards "shout out," telling us that life and the presence of God within us is much more important than the place where we live. Just as God cannot be contained in a temple or cathedral, so also your spirit and mine cannot be contained within the walls of our homes. We must pray and work earnestly to free ourselves from the bonds of "things."

Spiritual teachers have always taught that we should free ourselves from "attachments." Each of us must determine the ways in which the things around us interfere with our connection to God. Dorothy Day lived a life of simplicity and dedication. But she loved listening to the opera on Saturdays, and she found that great novels nourished her spirit. By celebrating these works of art, she and many other committed Christians have shown us that art, literature, and music can refresh and lift us up, bringing us closer to God. It is up to us to determine what elements of culture will serve best in bringing us closer to God and which are distractions.

REFLECTION AND WEEKLY PRACTICE

This week, think about the "stones" in your life—the buildings and places—of living, of travel, or of entertainment. How do these "temples" help or hinder your life with God? We are deeply rooted in our past. The architecture, the materials, the heating, and water systems all speak of generations even centuries of people who have worked to make your home what it is. You and I should be grateful for these connections—they shout to us of the human family. We are, under God, part of this great family and tradition. When the "stones shout out," it is sometimes to warn us and sometimes to remind us of our very real and positive connections.

22

An Unclean Spirit

*"What have you to do with us, Jesus of Nazareth? Have
you come to destroy us? I know who you are, the Holy
One of God." But Jesus rebuked him, saying, "Be silent,
and come out of him!"* [MARK 1:24-25]

This encounter between Jesus and an "unclean spirit"
takes place early in Mark's gospel. John baptized
Jesus, Satan tempted him, Jesus selected his first
disciples, and then came this remarkable encounter. Jesus
had indeed come to battle against evil. And here he meets his
adversary in a synagogue.

What are we to think of evil spirits, of Satan? The Old
Testament does not have much to say about Satan. For centuries Christians believed that the snake tempting Adam and
Eve was the devil in disguise. But more recently theologians
with great insight have come to view original sin, not as an
event long past, but as a kind of inescapable, pervasive evil
infecting all of us. The Genesis story is symbolic. Adrian
Hastings says that the tempter was simply a snake. A snake
that talked much in the way animals talk in children's stories.
But original sin is not to be taken lightly. Something has gone
very wrong.

In the Book of Job, Satan is something of an accuser, first coming into the discussion at God's invitation. God tells Satan to look at the just and upright man, Job. Satan does of course take up the challenge and with God's permission makes things worse and worse for Job. But he is not so much a tempter as one discussing earthly rewards and punishments and how they might relate to a good life—in ways not unlike the discussions that Christians have had and continue to have. Should we consider the good things of life as blessings from God? Is the lack or loss of these things a punishment from God?

Whatever we might think about the devil, as followers of Christ we do believe that good and evil are in combat—in our world and in our hearts. Like the unclean spirit confronting Jesus, our darker angels know how to call us by name, to flatter us, to pretend that something evil is really good.

Jesus encountered the unclean spirit in the synagogue. And might this happen in our parish community? An unclean spirit—in church? The first thing that might come to mind is the sexual abuse scandals that have plagued the Catholic Church. Or we might think of the greed that has so often entered religious activity as the desire for money gets in the way of gospel values. These are indeed evils—some of great magnitude—and we need to combat them. Some lay people and priests have shown extraordinary courage challenging bishops who have failed to protect innocent children.

But there are other evils, closer to home for most of us. I am thinking simply of gossip, perhaps harmless, perhaps not. It is so much a part of our lives, in and out of church, that we rarely reflect on it.

THE CHRISTIAN EXPERIENCE

The Letter of James has a good deal of practical wisdom. It talks about the harm that can be done through speech. The author suggests that a mighty ship is steered by a small rudder, and a giant forest may be set ablaze by a small fire. By analogy, we should recognize the power of the tongue— for good or ill. The author goes on to say that a mountain spring does not yield both fresh and brackish water. Rather, a pure spring sends forth pure water. We ought to "tame our tongues" so that we speak what is right and good.

REFLECTION AND WEEKLY PRACTICE

I think it can be useful for each of us to review our conversations and how we respond. Would we mind if the person we are talking about heard our conversation? If the answer is yes, then the embarrassment we would feel is probably a sign that we would do better not to make the comments. We are perhaps making them to make ourselves appear better by comparison.

Are these comments helpful to the person with whom we are talking? We should be in the business of strengthening and supporting one another, not somehow building ourselves up at the expense of others.

How is this conversation helpful to others? There are many ways in which positive words can help others. There are many people around you, in your community, your parish, and your family for whom a small amount of reassurance can go a very long way.

We should be wary of the unclean spirits within us. They can fool us, telling us to pretend that we are acknowledging God's grace when we are in fact promoting ourselves. Guarding our speech has an additional advantage in that we learn the power of language and will have the courage to use it when necessary to say things that are important but not popular.

⇒ 23 ⇐

We Tried
to Stop Him

*John answered, "Master, we saw someone casting out
demons in your name, and we tried to stop him, because
he does not follow with us." But Jesus said to him, "Do
not stop him; for whoever is not against you is for you."*

[LUKE 9:49–50]

Why is it that we have this deep-down tension,
conflict even, between our efforts to live in
peace with others across the boundaries of religion and ethnicity, and our need to dominate, to prove that
we are different and better, that our group is special? This
tension seems to be true, whether we consider ourselves as
individuals or as members of groups.

Pride in group is widespread, across nations and centuries. People often find a large measure of their identity in this
membership. It may be in country, ethnicity, club, or school,
and this kind of exclusive pride is very often found in religion. And then the reverse becomes important. If my group
is right, then your group is wrong. In matters of religion, the
stakes can be very high—so that each group wants to prevent

others from doing what they believe is required. We have heard it said that "Error has no rights."

Jesus was peculiarly free from this view and this way of acting. He was an observant Jew but remarkably unconcerned about some of the details regarding washings and diet. He was critical of those trying to enforce too many rules. As Christians, we have devised regulations and tried hard to show that these requirements, in some way or other, go back to Jesus.

The Catholic Church has taught that there are seven sacraments, instituted by Christ. But locating the founding situations and statements has been problematic. The more common teaching now is that the sacraments have come about through the church guided by the Spirit, and through Christ still with us. The Protestant churches, with a very strong emphasis on Scripture, have generally accepted only two sacraments, baptism and the Eucharist.

It is always difficult to speculate about something that is not there: Jesus did not provide lengthy rules and regulations. Surely this was a way open to him. Consider the Book of Leviticus, of which he was aware. In chapter 2 we read:

> When anyone presents a grain offering to the LORD, the offering shall be of choice flour; the worshiper shall pour oil on it, and put frankincense on it, and bring it to Aaron's sons the priests. After taking from it a handful of the choice flour and oil, with all its frankincense, the priest shall turn this token portion into smoke on the altar, an offering by fire of pleasing odor to the LORD. [LEVITICUS 2:1-2]

This is a small fragment of the directives about sacrifices, which is only a small part of the directives that cover many other areas: the dietary laws, for example, take a great deal of space. Consider by contrast the simplicity and brevity of Jesus at the Last Supper:

> While they were eating, Jesus took a loaf of bread, and after blessing it he broke it, gave it to the disciples, and said, "Take, eat; this is my body." Then he took a cup, and after giving thanks, he gave it to them, saying, "Drink from it, all of you; for this is my blood of the covenant, which is poured out for many for the forgiveness of sins." [MATTHEW 26:26–28]

There is a simplicity and even informality here that we must think was deliberate. And so, following our best understandings, we of different traditions have taken different routes in following Jesus' example and instruction. In the gospel accounts we don't even find the directive, "Do this in remembrance of me." This is in Paul's account.

THE CHRISTIAN EXPERIENCE

Looking back over our shared history, we of the Christian church or churches—I am not sure which is more accurate—have a great deal to be embarrassed and even ashamed about. One of our greatest sins is the fragmentation of the community. We have at many times and in many ways tried to stop one another, as the disciples proudly reported back to Jesus that they were doing.

Consider Luther. He was a priest, Scripture scholar, and teacher. He saw abuses. The pope and his delegates claimed the power not only to teach but, with payment, through offerings of money, to wash away the effects of sin so that the living and the dead might more easily find heaven. Luther was rightly scandalized; he condemned indulgences, and as time went on he taught that the pope and bishops had no power at all over the consciences of Christians. Scripture is enough.

Luther became a pastor and leader, separate from the Catholic Church. Even before Luther, Christianity had begun fragmenting into many competing sects. These groups sought and often received the protection of princes and local governments. And soon the slogan was heard: "Whoever has power over the region, selects the religion." Religious wars ensued. For centuries, Catholics and Protestants were enemies. Each opposed violently the other's theology, rituals, and teachings about what it means to follow Christ.

Of course, in the exchange between Jesus and his followers that we are discussing, the disciples did not seem to use violence. "We tried to stop him" seems to mean a verbal encounter. Jesus told them not to do even this.

REFLECTION

What can we learn from this encounter after these many centuries? Perhaps in a more general way, beyond Christianity, we learn that it does not help to silence people. Usually in a dispute there is truth on both sides and an honest discussion can be beneficial. As is generally the case, Jesus is far ahead of us.

The teaching church has proceeded well when it has permitted the healthy exchange of ideas. The study of Scripture is a good example—at least in recent years. Beginning with Pius XII, the Catholic Church began, cautiously at first and then with greater confidence, to open the doors of Scripture study—using language expertise, historical and anthropological criticism, along with a variety of other methods. Scholars of varied Christian traditions worked together, looking carefully into the words and expressions of Scripture.

WEEKLY PRACTICE

Like Jesus himself, we can say that the words of Scripture are fully human and fully divine. The meanings of Scripture are complex, but when approached with a prayerful mind and heart, Scripture will nourish and sustain us. If you do not read Scripture regularly, consider it. You will be rewarded! You might start with the Acts of the Apostles: a dramatic narrative about how the church, under the power of the Spirit, got started.

≈ **24** ≈

What Is Truth

Pilate asked him, "So you are a king?" Jesus answered,
"You say that I am a king. For this I was born, and
for this I came into the world, to testify to the truth.
Everyone who belongs to the truth listens to my voice."
Pilate asked him, "What is truth?" [JOHN 18:37-38]

In each of the four gospels, Pilate asks Jesus the question, "Are you a king?" In the first three gospels, Jesus replies, "You say so." In the Gospel of John, the answer is almost the same. The fact that the question is found in all the gospels gives added weight to the exchange, and Christians have debated the meaning of the response.

Jesus was brought to Pilate because he was gaining influence among the people, and the Jewish leaders knew that the Romans would not tolerate challenges to their rule. So for them to say he claimed to be a king would surely get Pilate's attention. And Pilate, like interrogators of every century, wanted a confession. It makes judgment easier.

Perhaps by saying, "You say that I am a king," Jesus is trying to force the issue. Pilate is depicted in the gospels as uncertain. He tries to change the conversation and then reluctantly passes judgment. In Matthew's gospel he tries to escape responsibility: he washes his hands, declaring "I am innocent of this man's blood," while condemning him to death.

Jesus does accept the title but on his terms, telling Pilate that his mission is to testify to the truth. This is another shift in expectations; the work of a king is not usually to testify; it is to rule. But in the Gospel of John we are drawn into courtroom-like proceedings, with witnesses and testimonies. The Prologue says that John came as a witness to the truth. Later, we are told that the Father bears witness (5:30). Later still, Jesus says that the Spirit will testify about him (15:26). In the passage we are discussing, Jesus says that he himself testifies to the truth.

Then we have Pilate's well-known response, "What is truth?"

A statement is true when it correctly describes what exists in the world around and beyond us. If I say, "There is a maple tree next to my house," you can come to visit and see that this is true. If I say, "I have visited Rome," well, for this you will have to take my word, although I could show you pictures.

Truth is of great importance in matters of law and justice. Even those of evil intent try to get confessions from the ones they accuse, because there is widespread belief in the importance of speaking the truth. Scientists, whether or not they believe in God, have strong beliefs that statements about the world can be shown to be true or not.

THE CHRISTIAN EXPERIENCE

Bernard Lonergan, a Jesuit philosopher and theologian, discussed different views of the world around us: what he called descriptive and explanatory. Every day the sun rises in the east and sets in the west. You can find the times for sunrise and sunset where you live. We find it in a different location at three in the afternoon than at ten in the morning. And that is an accurate description of what is happening. The earth seems quite solid, stationary, and even flat. But we know our earth is a sphere that rotates on its axis and also moves through space. Although the sun also moves through space, what we see as its movement is really due to the rotation of the earth.

So it turns out that finding truth is something we, as a community, as humankind, must work at. Each generation seeks to build on what had come before. Truth is not always what it had seemed to be.

The leaders of all of the Christian churches have had an unfortunate tendency to think that truth can be legislated. Based on the Bible or on theological principles they have at times made the age of the universe or the movement of the earth matters of doctrine. Fortunately science and theology are continually finding surprises, finding that the search for truth is endless and boundless. The finding that the sun is at the center of the solar system was at first difficult to reconcile with human's thinking of what is important in God's plan. But it seems wonderful that we like Jesus can bear witness to the truth.

REFLECTION

Perhaps we can learn lessons about truth in religious matters from the quest for truth in other areas. Perhaps the church, as teacher, has been too insistent in believing that it possesses and teaches ultimate truth. We seek the truth, whether as scientists, human beings, or believers. But for us limited humans, truth is always partial and provisional, never final. We in community are always discovering new ways of seeing and believing. And in this process we become witnesses to the truth as it emerges within us and among us.

WEEKLY PRACTICE

Jesus said that those who belong to the truth hear his voice. I think that "belonging to the truth" is a lifelong project. We have to put aside our prejudices and biases. As we become more open to the truth, Christ our Lord will find us. As we listen to his voice in Scripture, in the lives of those around us, and through prayer, we participate more fully in the life of God. This week consider and, as time permits, write down how your own quest for truth has proceeded.

⇒ **25** ⇐

The Traditions of the Elders

Now when the Pharisees and some of the scribes who had come from Jerusalem gathered around him, they noticed that some of his disciples were eating with defiled hands, that is, without washing them....So the Pharisees and the scribes asked him, "Why do your disciples not live according to the tradition of the elders, but eat with defiled hands?"...Then he said to them, "You have a fine way of rejecting the commandment of God in order to keep your tradition!" [MARK 7:1-2, 5, 9]

This exchange seems archaic and out-of-step with today's concerns. We think that, of course, Jesus was aware of the formulaic, tradition-bound thinking and the kinds of rituals that the Jewish religious leaders imposed. We, after all these centuries, are enlightened. We know that Jesus' spiritual and universal understandings transcended the "traditions of the elders." And we are the heirs of his more enlightened thinking.

But perhaps the conversation was more integral to Jesus' concerns and his mission than we think. Further on in this exchange, Jesus says that his questioners reject the commandments of God while keeping their own interpretations, and he goes on to give an example. Jesus quotes the commandment, "Honor your father and mother," and then points to a practice, apparently common at the time, of avoiding support for parents by declaring the money an offering to God while also retaining use of it. The "offering" was a legal fiction.

Again, we might ask how this applies to us. What was Jesus saying? It seems he was pointing to the importance of conscience. He goes on to say that washing dishes is not important. Evil arises from the heart. How does Jesus' appeal to conscience apply to us?

THE CHRISTIAN EXPERIENCE

Fr. James Keenan offers a number of insights in his summary article on conscience (*America*, 1/2/17). He reports that in the years since World War II moral theologians in Europe have taken a different direction from those in America. In particular, those in Europe have acknowledged the communal and individual guilt that they incurred through the atrocities of war and the Holocaust. This recognition of sin has provided a fresh appreciation of God's love and the meaning of faith. His discussion brings to mind Dietrich Bonhoeffer's consideration of "cheap grace" in which the would-be Christian accepts Christ without the commitment and determination to act in a Christ-like way.

Fr. Keenan suggests among other things that we consider "American Exceptionalism." The idea, although not the expression, began in the seventeenth century with the Puritan leader John Winthrop, who spoke of how a city on a hill cannot be hidden, a phrase from Matthew's gospel. In his writings Winthrop said he wanted the Puritan community to set an example in its Christian behavior, its concern for others, and its prayerful way of life.

As time passed, however, the phrase "city on a hill" and American Exceptionalism came to express a certain religious/national pride, undergirding the belief that the Unites States is better than other countries and not subject to the same norms and requirements. In recent years, presidents have used the phrase "city on a hill" to express the special nature of America's mission.

The term "Manifest Destiny" is another name for this specialness. The thinking was that if people came here for religious freedom, looking to worship God, and they found vast resources in arable, livable land and water, then surely God must have intended this people to possess this great land. As the nation grew and became stronger, its "destiny" became larger and grander.

What does this all mean to us?

Violence. We are the heirs of "the traditions of the elders." We participate in and are complicit in a violent and militaristic tradition. From the killing of native peoples, to the pursuit of slavery, through atomic bombs, and on to our recent wars and military interventions and our vast armament industry, we are a nation ready to threaten and quick to use violence.

Greed. The acquisition of wealth in all its forms is a curse on modern society. But as with violence, the United States seems to accept and encourage greed more than many other nations. Capitalism has certain merit: the division of labor, specialization, and perhaps some forms of competition can be productive. But capitalism also has many faults in the exploitation of land and in unjust practices in which a few make exorbitant amounts of money. All of this generally hurts others. And then there is the day-to-day greed in business and personal transactions that is generally accepted. Greed is another tradition of the elders.

REFLECTION

The problem with these and other characteristics of contemporary life is that they have been, in many ways, accepted by and even blessed by the Christian churches. Flags are often found in churches; on occasion we sing patriotic songs during worship. We celebrate soldiers and veterans. Their presence at certain events adds solemnity to our church services. We believe that whatever violence we use is acceptable because it is necessary. Are we neglecting the commandment "Thou shalt not kill" while accepting the "traditions of the elders"?

WEEKLY PRACTICE

Consider whether your patriotism is in conflict with your life and beliefs as a Christian. Think about how being a Christian should lift us beyond national pride. Consider how and in what ways you accept or condone the violence and greed that are part of the modern world. Think and pray about how Christ wants us to live our lives in love and service. What are you doing now and how can you best imitate Christ this week?